Shadow Work Journal and Workbook

Real and Proven Strategies for Addressing Trauma, Healing Your inner Child, and Integrating Your Shadow Self

Sophie Ashford

© Copyright 2025 – Sophie Ashford - All rights reserved

The content within this book may not be reproduced, duplicated, or transmitted without direct written permission from the author or the publisher.

Under no circumstances will any blame or legal responsibility be held against the publisher, or author, for any damages, reparation, or monetary loss due to the information contained within this book, either directly or indirectly.

Legal Notice

This book is copyright protected. This book is only for personal use. You cannot amend, distribute, sell, use, quote, or paraphrase any part, or the content within this book, without the consent of the author-publisher.

Disclaimer Notice

Please note that the information contained within this document is for educational and entertainment purposes only. All effort has been executed to present accurate, up-to-date, and reliable, complete information. No warranties of any kind are declared or implied. Readers acknowledge that the author is not engaging in the rendering of legal, financial, medical, or professional advice.

Table of Contents

Introduction 5

Part 1: Understanding Shadow Work 11

The Concept of the Shadow Self 12

Identifying the Shadow 16

The Benefits of Shadow Work 21

Carl Jung's Four Main Archetypes 26

Understanding How Your Shadow Works 31

Disarming the Inner Critic 36

Connecting with Your Inner Child 41

Transforming Anger and Shame 46

Part 2: Exercises and Techniques for Shadow Work 51

Mindfulness Meditation Guide 52

Creative Art Therapy Activities 54

Narrative Writing Exercises 57

Guided Imagery Practice 60

Role-Playing Scenarios 62

Breathwork Practices 65

Affirmation Crafting and Reflection 68

Body Scanning Activity 72

Emotional Freedom Technique 75

Inner Child Healing Exercises 78

Visualization Techniques 81

Somatic Experiencing Tasks 83

Cognitive Restructuring Exercises 85

Progressive Muscle Relaxation Guide 87

Sound Healing Guide 89

Shadow Integration Rituals 91

Gratitude Practices 93

The Power of Shared Journeys 95

Part 3: Shadow Work Prompts 96

Prompts for Trauma 97

Prompts for Career and Workplace 99

Prompts for Spirituality 101

Prompts for Relationships 103

Prompts for Self-Esteem and Self-Worth 105

Prompts for Body Image 107

Prompts for Mental Health and Well-Being 109

Prompts for Childhood Memories and Upbringing 111

Prompts for Grief and Loss 113

Prompts for Personal Development and Growth 115

Prompts for Social and Cultural Conditioning 117

Prompts for Fear and Anxiety 119

Prompts for Anger and Forgiveness 121

Prompts for Future Aspirations and Anxieties 123

Prompts for Financial Beliefs and Behaviors 125

Prompts for Health and Wellness 127

Prompts for Creativity and Expression 129

Prompts for Decision Making and Regrets 131

Prompts for Boundaries and Personal Space 133

Prompts for Dreams and Subconscious Thoughts 135

Part 4: Triggers Identification 137

Part 5: Integrating the Shadow 140

Acceptance and Compassion 141

Forgiveness & Letting Go 147

Conscious Tension Release 153

Processing Your Pain 157

Transformation and Growth 161

Maintaining Balance 167

Finding the Path to Non-Situational Happiness 170

A Beacon for Fellow Travelers 172

Conclusion 173

About the Author 174

Introduction

Every once in a while, we all encounter a moment that jolts us out of our regular routine, forcing us to confront the deeper, darker parts of ourselves. Imagine this: you're sitting in your car after a long day at work, the rain gently tapping on the roof. The radio plays a song, a melancholic melody that takes you back to a moment you had forgotten. Suddenly, a well of emotion rises from within, and you're taken aback by the unexpected tears blurring your vision. You wonder, why now? Why this song? Why this memory? What lies in the shadows of our mind, stirring these potent emotions, and why do we so often overlook them?

Life is a whirlwind of events, responsibilities, and distractions. From the time we wake up to the moment we lay our heads down at night, we are bombarded with a barrage of tasks, demands, and stimuli. And while we navigate through this daily hustle, there are parts of us – thoughts, feelings, and memories – that get pushed to the background. These hidden facets of our existence, often concealed by our conscious minds, start to shape our actions, reactions, and even our self-worth, without us realizing.

How many times have you found yourself reacting to a situation more intensely than it warranted? Or feeling inexplicably low without any discernible reason? The pain of past traumas, suppressed anxieties, and unacknowledged desires lurk beneath the surface, driving these bewildering responses. We're left feeling disconnected, not only from the world around us but, more critically, from ourselves. This chasm, between who we believe we are and the entirety of our being, is the root of many problems we face in our daily lives: unexpected bouts of anger, inexplicable sadness, fears, inhibitions, and even self-sabotage.

In the maze of our busy lives, we often yearn for a compass, a guiding light that can help us navigate the intricate pathways of our psyche. This longing isn't just about seeking external guidance but about unlocking a map that already exists within us, one that can lead us to clarity, understanding, and healing.

Consider the moments when nature, in all her wisdom, whispers her secrets to those who listen. Like a forest that flourishes after a wildfire, our minds too possess the incredible power of rejuvenation and growth. But, just as the forest needs the sun, rain, and soil to heal, our minds require attention, understanding, and care. The hidden emotions, memories, and desires aren't merely obstacles; they are signposts, guiding us toward a more profound understanding of ourselves. By acknowledging and confronting these shadowy facets, we unlock doors to uncharted territories of our psyche, leading to a richer, more fulfilling life experience.

It's not about erasing past traumas or suppressing emotions. It's about weaving them into the tapestry of our lives in a way that adds depth, meaning, and strength. Through this journey, you won't just find solutions to problems you're aware of; you'll discover parts of you that you didn't know existed, facets that have been waiting for the light of acknowledgment to shine and enrich your existence.

Imagine standing at the edge of a vast, untapped gold mine. Every step you take from here on is a stride towards unlocking treasures that hold the power to transform your life. This journey is not just about self-discovery but about sculpting a life of purpose, passion, and unparalleled vibrancy.

By diving deep into the layers of your subconscious, you'll begin to:

1. *Achieve clarity*: Understand the reasons behind your actions and emotions, helping you navigate life's challenges with poise.

2. *Build resilience*: Recognize patterns from your past that no longer serve you and replace them with new, empowering beliefs.

3. *Enhance relationships*: By understanding yourself better, you'll foster deeper connections with others, enriching both personal and professional relationships.

4. *Harness untapped potential*: With newfound self-awareness, barriers that once seemed insurmountable will begin to crumble, making way for growth and opportunities.

5. *Live with purpose*: Align your actions and goals with your authentic self, driving both fulfillment and success.

By confronting and embracing the shadows within, you are taking a bold step towards a life that resonates with authenticity and joy. The answers you seek are not beyond the horizon but deep within you, waiting to be unveiled, acknowledged, and celebrated.

The journey you're about to embark on is based on years of meticulous exploration, observation, and firsthand experience. While the realm of the subconscious, the shadows within, might seem nebulous, the path laid out for you is grounded in practical wisdom. This is not just another self-help fad or a fly-by-night solution. The methods and insights presented have been distilled from a wealth of personal encounters, real-life stories, and countless hours spent navigating the intricate corridors of the human psyche.

You might wonder why this particular approach, why this particular path? It's simple: because it has stood the test of time. Many before you have walked this path, confronting their shadows, understanding them, and emerging on the other side with a richer, more profound sense of self. Their transformation, their testimonials, and their newfound zest for life serve as a testament to the power and efficacy of the process outlined in this guide.

In a world brimming with quick fixes and superficial solutions, what you have before you is a deep dive into the very essence of your being. It's not about skimming the surface but about diving deep, exploring, understanding, and emerging with treasures that have the power to transform your life in ways you've only dreamed of.

While every individual's journey is unique, there exists a universal truth that binds us all: the desire for understanding, connection, and purpose. As you traverse the pathways of your psyche, a transformative experience awaits. Each page turned, each exercise completed, and each reflection pondered will steadily guide you towards a place of self-awareness and empowerment.

As you delve deeper into your shadows, there will be moments of revelation, moments when the fog of confusion lifts to reveal landscapes of clarity. There will be instances when old wounds are brought to light, not to inflict pain, but to heal and fortify. And as you progress, the scattered pieces of your life's puzzle will start aligning, crafting a picture of profound beauty and meaning.

You don't merely embark on a journey of discovery; you embark on a path of transformation. Embracing your shadows isn't just about confronting the hidden or the suppressed; it's about reclaiming the fragments of yourself that hold the keys to your fullest potential. By the end of this journey, not only will you understand yourself better, but you'll also find yourself equipped to navigate life's twists and turns with grace, resilience, and authenticity.

Imagine standing at a crossroads, the sun setting on one horizon and the dawn breaking on the other. Time, as we know, is the one resource we can't reclaim, and with every passing moment, opportunities for growth, healing, and transformation are either seized or missed.

The magic, the potential, and the promise of a more profound connection with oneself shouldn't be deferred for a distant 'someday.' Every day that we shy away from confronting our innermost thoughts and feelings is another day we deprive ourselves of living our most authentic, fulfilled lives. The cost of inaction isn't just the missed chance of today, but the ripple effect it has on our tomorrows.

Can you truly afford to wait any longer? To let another day, week, or year slip by, shackled by the uncertainties and fears of the unknown? The promise of a life lived in tune with your deepest desires, free from the chains of past traumas and unresolved emotions, is right at your fingertips. The power to transform, to break free, and to soar to new heights is not in some distant future but here, now, within these pages and within yourself.

The question is, will you seize this moment, this opportunity, this gift, and step into the light of understanding and transformation? Or will you let the shadows grow longer, allowing them to shape your destiny?

In times past, the quest for self-understanding was often a solitary, arduous journey. Individuals would spend years, sometimes even lifetimes, seeking answers to their innermost queries, often wandering aimlessly in a maze of confusion and despair. Ancient civilizations built monasteries on remote mountaintops, and seekers would isolate themselves, dedicating years in solitude, hoping to find a glimmer of clarity. Even in more recent times, many have felt trapped, navigating the labyrinth of their minds without a guide, map, or compass.

While the human quest for understanding is as old as time itself, the tools and methods have often been shrouded in mystery, reserved for the select few who could access them. The rest were left to grapple in the dark, yearning for a beacon of light. The feelings of frustration, of being on the verge of a breakthrough but not quite getting there, are sentiments many have known all too well.

Imagine trying to assemble a puzzle without knowing the final picture, or navigating a dense forest without a map. That's how the journey into the self used to be—overwhelming, filled with trial and error, and, for many, a sense of hopelessness at not finding the answers they so desperately sought.

But what if you didn't have to walk this path alone? What if, instead of blindly searching, you were handed a map, one that had been refined and perfected over time, marked with signposts to guide your way? This is the promise of the information contained within this book – a culmination of age-old wisdom and contemporary insights, offering a clear, structured path towards self-realization and transformation.

Life has a curious way of leading us to the exact places, experiences, and insights we need at precisely the right moment. It's as if the universe conspires in our favor, nudging us gently toward the paths that hold the most promise for our growth. As you hold this book, you might feel a familiar resonance, an unspoken connection, a quiet whisper that says, "This is what I've been searching for."

Every chapter, every exercise, every reflection within these pages seems to echo your thoughts, your questions, your yearnings. It's not mere coincidence; it's a testament to the universality of the human experience. And while each of our journeys is unique, the underlying threads of emotion, discovery, and transformation are remarkably similar.

Perhaps you've skimmed through countless books, attended workshops, or sought guidance in various forms, only to feel a void, a sense that something was missing. But with this guide, it feels different. The words resonate, the exercises seem tailored for you, and the insights strike a chord deep within. It's as if the book speaks directly to your soul, addressing your unique challenges, aspirations, and dreams.

Envision a life where your past doesn't dictate your future, where every shadow is an opportunity for growth, and where understanding oneself is the key to unlocking a world of potential. That vision, that promise, is within reach. And this, dear reader, might just be the guide you've been waiting for, the catalyst that propels you into a journey of profound discovery and transformation.

Part 1:
Understanding Shadow Work

Delve into the profound world of the shadow self, a concept that has intrigued thinkers, psychologists, and seekers of self-awareness for ages. In this enlightening first part, we embark on a comprehensive exploration of the shadow, laying a robust foundation for the chapters that follow. We commence with the philosophical underpinnings, tracing back to the revolutionary insights of Carl Jung. Jung's theories form the bedrock upon which the modern understanding of the shadow stands, illuminating its hidden crevices and offering clarity.

As you move forward, you'll delve into the multifaceted nature of the shadow, witnessing its manifestations in various aspects of life. This journey isn't just about recognition but about understanding the intricate dance of emotions, feelings, and memories that the shadow weaves. We explore emotions from the raw intensity of anger to the subtle nuances of shame, each intertwined with the shadow's enigmatic presence.

But identifying the shadow is only the tip of the iceberg. It's essential to understand its roots, its triggers, and its influence on behavior and thought patterns. By exploring its relationship with our inner critic, connections to our cherished inner child, and its transformative power, this part equips you with the knowledge and wisdom to embrace the shadow, not as an adversary, but as an integral part of the self, waiting to be acknowledged and integrated.

Prepare to challenge existing beliefs, to question, to introspect, and most importantly, to grow. This section sets the groundwork, ensuring you're primed and ready for the transformative exercises and introspections that lie in the subsequent parts.

The Concept of the Shadow Self

Have you ever caught yourself reacting in a way that seemed out of character? A sudden burst of anger, an unexpected bout of jealousy, or perhaps a moment of irrational fear? These reactions, often surprising even to ourselves, are not anomalies. They are whispers from a part of our psyche that often remains hidden, even from our conscious selves. This part is what Carl Jung, the Swiss psychiatrist, termed as the "Shadow Self." The concept of the Shadow Self finds its roots in Jungian psychology. Carl Jung believed that as we grow and adapt to societal norms and expectations, we tend to suppress certain aspects of our personality. These suppressed parts don't just vanish; they form a reservoir of our unexpressed emotions, desires, and traits. This reservoir is the Shadow. It's not just a collection of our so-called 'negative' traits but also houses potentialities that haven't found an expression in our conscious life.

Imagine a room filled with objects, representing different facets of your personality. The room has a single source of light. The objects directly under this light are the traits, behaviors, and emotions you're aware of – the ones you identify with. But what about the objects lurking in the shadows, just beyond the light's reach? They are still part of the room, part of you, but often remain unseen. It's essential to understand that the Shadow isn't inherently evil or negative. It's neutral. It contains both the traits we deem undesirable and those we might see as positive but haven't fully integrated into our conscious self. For instance, a person might suppress their assertiveness due to early life experiences, and this trait then becomes a part of their shadow.

Acknowledging the Shadow Self is the first step towards holistic self-awareness. By turning a blind eye, we risk being controlled by it. Unacknowledged shadows can manifest in unexpected ways, influencing our behaviors, relationships, and even our life choices. But by recognizing and embracing it, we open the door to profound self-understanding and growth. So, as you journey through these pages, remember: the Shadow isn't an enemy to be defeated. It's a part of you, waiting to be understood and integrated. And this journey, while challenging, promises to be one of the most rewarding ones you'll ever undertake.

In the dance of self-discovery, the shadow self is not a solo performer but rather engages in a duet with the conscious self. It is a dance of light and dark, known and unknown, seen and unseen. The shadow is not a separate entity but rather an integral part of the whole self, embodying the dual nature of our existence. This duality is not about a battle between good and evil, as often portrayed in literature and media. It is more nuanced, a complex interplay of contrasting elements that exist within each one of us. The shadow contains aspects that we might label as 'negative' – anger, jealousy, fear – but it also holds 'positive' elements – untapped potentials, unexpressed talents, and overlooked strengths.

Imagine a tree. Its branches reach out, basking in the sunlight, visible and acknowledged. But beneath the surface, its roots spread out in the dark soil, unseen yet vital. They anchor the tree, nourish it, and contribute to its growth in ways that the branches alone cannot. The shadow self is akin to these roots, hidden yet essential, feared yet powerful.

Yet, it's not a realm of absolute darkness. Within the shadow, there are slivers of light, fragments of our unexpressed 'positive' traits that we've suppressed or overlooked. Perhaps it's the creativity stifled in childhood, the compassion tempered by a harsh experience, or the leadership potential muted by self-doubt. The shadow is not just a storehouse of our fears and insecurities but also a treasure trove of strengths and talents waiting to be acknowledged and integrated. As we delve deeper into subsequent chapters, we will explore this duality in detail, unraveling the intricate dance between light and dark, conscious and unconscious. We will journey into the depths of the shadow, not with trepidation but with curiosity, not to vanquish but to embrace, for in the heart of darkness, there lies a light untapped, a potential unexplored.

As we pull back the curtain to reveal the enigmatic dance of the shadow self, a realization dawns: the journey to self-discovery is incomplete without traversing the hidden corridors of our inner world. The shadow, with its enigmatic presence, is not a distant, isolated island but a continent rich in undiscovered terrains, woven intricately into the fabric of our being.

The shadow self is not a detour on our journey but a path that leads us to the core of our existence. It's a silent whisper of our unspoken fears, unacknowledged strengths, and unexpressed potentials. To ignore it is to silence a part of our soul, to live a life not fully realized, a song not entirely sung. Yet, the acknowledgment of the shadow is not an endpoint but a beginning. It's the first step into a world where light and dark dance in unison, where the known and unknown embrace each other. It's a gateway to a more profound, holistic self-awareness, a journey from fragmentation to wholeness.

In the chapters that follow, we will not only explore but also learn to embrace this duality. We will unravel the threads of the shadow with compassion, understanding, and curiosity. We will learn that in the dance of self-discovery, every step, every movement, every breath is an intricate blend of light and dark. And in this dance, we find our most authentic, unfiltered self. As you turn the pages, remember, the shadow is not a specter to be feared but a companion on our journey. It's a mirror reflecting the parts of us waiting to step into the light, a voice echoing the silent whispers of our soul. In the dance of shadows, we don't just find our fears and insecurities but also our strengths, potentials, and the unutterable beauty of our entire being.

Reflecting Questions

What emotions or reactions arise when you consider the existence of your shadow self, and what insights do these feelings provide about your unexplored or unacknowledged aspects?

_____
_____
_____
_____
_____
_____

In what ways have you noticed the dual nature of your shadow manifesting in your behaviors, thoughts, or emotions, and how can acknowledging this duality contribute to your personal growth?

_____

_____

_____

_____

How might your life transform if you were to fully embrace and integrate the hidden elements of your shadow into your conscious self?

_____

_____

_____

_____

Reflect on a moment where your shadow self might have influenced your actions or decisions. What can this specific instance reveal about the suppressed or unexpressed aspects of your personality?

_____

_____

_____

_____

Identifying the Shadow

The journey into the depths of the shadow self is akin to stepping into a room where echoes of an enigmatic melody linger. Each note, a fragment of the self, veiled in mystery, waiting to be uncovered, acknowledged, and embraced. But how does one begin to discern these hidden notes? How do we unveil the melodies of the shadow that dance silently in the recesses of our soul?

The first step is observation - a vigilant, yet gentle scrutiny of our reactions, behaviors, and emotions. It's akin to being a silent witness to the unfolding drama of our inner world. When a sudden surge of emotion takes hold, or an unexpected reaction emerges, pause. In this pause, lies the gateway to the shadow. Consider a practical exercise of maintaining a 'Shadow Journal'. In this sacred space, record instances where emotions and reactions surprised you. Was there a sudden burst of anger? An unexpected wave of sadness? A flicker of jealousy? Note them down without judgment, for judgment is the veil that obscures the shadow. As you document these moments, patterns begin to emerge. These patterns are like the threads that weave the intricate tapestry of the shadow self. Each thread, a clue; each pattern, a revelation of the hidden aspects that reside in the silent corridors of the soul.

Another powerful tool is reflection. Dedicate moments of solitude to delve into these documented instances. Ask yourself - "Why did this emotion emerge? What triggered this reaction?" It's not about finding immediate answers but about asking the questions. For in the realm of the shadow, questions are the lanterns that illuminate the hidden paths. Engage in conversations with the self. Dialogues that are honest, raw, and unfiltered. Imagine sitting across a version of yourself, and in this intimate encounter, let the questions flow. "Why does criticism evoke a storm of defensiveness? Why does abandonment stir the oceans of anxiety?" In these dialogues, listen. Listen not just to the words, but to the silences, the pauses, the unuttered, for the shadow speaks in whispers, in the silent notes of the unsung melodies.

In this exploration, dreams become allies. The nocturnal journeys of the soul, where symbols, images, and narratives emerge from the depths of the unconscious. Maintain a 'Dream Diary'.

Record the enigmatic narratives of your dreams, for they are the echoes of the shadow, the silent songs of the unexpressed, the unacknowledged. In this process of observation, documentation, reflection, and exploration, the outlines of the shadow begin to emerge from the depths of obscurity. It's not a revelation that's stark or abrupt, but a gentle unfolding, like the first rays of the dawn that illuminate the landscapes shrouded in darkness.

Remember, this journey is not about confrontation but about a tender embrace. It's about holding space for the silent notes of the soul to emerge into the symphony of our existence. It's a dance of revelation, where each step, each note, each echo, unveils the melodies of the shadow - silent, yet profound; hidden, yet omnipresent. In this dance, we don't just encounter the shadow; we embrace the entirety of our being, in all its intricate, enigmatic, and beautiful melodies.

A Real-Life Scenario

Alice, a dedicated mother and a successful entrepreneur, found herself in the midst of a scenario that left her perplexed. One evening, as her daughter enthusiastically showcased her artwork, Alice's response was not one of admiration or encouragement, but a sharp critique, a detailed analysis of imperfections. The coldness in her voice was alien, not just to her daughter but to Alice herself. In another part of the world, David, known for his calm demeanor, found his hands trembling with an inexplicable rage during a casual conversation with a colleague. The trigger was insignificant, yet the eruption of anger was monumental. It was as if a dormant volcano within him had awakened, its existence unknown even to David. These instances, though distinct, are united by a common thread - the emergence of the shadow. It's not an orchestrated revelation but an unplanned, often unexpected unveiling. The shadow doesn't announce its arrival. It emerges in the silences, in the pauses, in the unguarded moments of our existence. For Alice, the critique of her daughter's artwork was not a reflection of the child's abilities but a voice echoing the unhealed wounds of Alice's own childhood, where perfection was not a pursuit but a requirement. In that moment of critique, it wasn't the mother speaking to the daughter but the wounded child speaking through the adult. David's uncharacteristic rage was not a response to his colleague's words but an eruption of suppressed emotions, a legacy of years of silencing his voice, muting his emotions, and burying his authentic expressions beneath the façade of calmness. In that moment of trembling anger, the buried emotions found a voice, the muted expressions a language.

The shadow emerges not in isolation but in relation to others, in interactions, in relationships. It's in the mirror of the 'other' that the shadow finds its reflection. It's not an enemy lurking in the corners but a companion walking beside us, its presence revealed in the mirrors of our relationships, interactions, and expressions. Yet, the emergence of the shadow is not a catastrophe but an opportunity. For Alice, the uncharacteristic coldness was a gateway to the unexplored terrains of her inner world, an invitation to heal the wounds of the child within. For David, the trembling rage was a call to acknowledge the suppressed emotions, an opportunity to give voice to the silent echoes of his soul. The shadow is not a sinister force but a silent companion. Its emergence is not a revelation of our imperfections but an invitation to wholeness. It unveils not to shame but to heal, not to critique but to complete. As we journey through the landscapes of our existence, let us remember - every Alice has her moments of uncharacteristic coldness; every David, his instances of trembling rage. Yet, in these moments, we are not encountering our imperfections but our completeness. For the shadow is not an intruder but a companion, not an enemy but an ally, not a revelation of our brokenness but an invitation to our wholeness. In its silent echoes, we find not just the unuttered notes of our soul but the symphony of our complete, unfiltered, and beautiful existence.

Initial Coping Strategies

In the quietude of introspection, where the whispers of the shadow self become audible, there lies a pivotal juncture. It's a space where the unveiled aspects of the self, those fragments that have long resided in obscurity, seek acknowledgment. Here, coping isn't about suppression or alteration, but about a gentle, compassionate embrace.

Consider Sarah, who, amidst a gathering of friends, felt an inexplicable wave of anxiety. The laughter and chatter around her seemed distant, as if she were an observer, not a participant. In that moment of isolation, amidst the crowd, the shadow whispered. Sarah's initial impulse was to suppress, to silence the anxiety. But suppression is a dam; it holds for a while, but eventually, the suppressed finds its voice, often with an intensified echo. Instead, Sarah chose acknowledgment. She excused herself, stepped into a space of solitude, and allowed the anxiety to speak. She didn't judge or analyze; she listened. In this listening, there was an acknowledgment, not just of the anxiety but of the shadow's whisper, the unexpressed, the suppressed. One of the initial coping strategies lies in this acknowledgment. It's about creating a space where the shadow isn't an intruder but a guest, welcomed and heard. It's not about an immediate resolution but about a patient, compassionate listening.

Another strategy is expression. Mark, a corporate executive, often found a storm of anger brewing within him. The triggers were trivial, yet the storm was tumultuous. One evening, amidst a storm, Mark chose a different path. He picked up a brush and began to paint. The canvas became the space where the storm found expression. Each stroke of the brush was a note of the shadow's silent song, each hue, a whisper of the unexpressed. Expression is a bridge. It connects the islands of suppression to the continents of acknowledgment. It's not about articulating the perfect words or creating the perfect art but about allowing the shadow a voice, a language, an expression.

Yet, another pivotal strategy is the cultivation of self-compassion. The journey into the shadow isn't a descent into the dungeons but a walk into the sanctuaries of the soul. It's a space where the fragmented finds wholeness, where the suppressed finds a voice. In this journey, self-compassion is the lantern. It illuminates the paths shrouded in judgment, criticism, and shame. When James encountered the silent echoes of abandonment issues, his initial response was self-criticism. But criticism is a wall; it isolates, separates. James chose to dismantle the wall. He embraced self-compassion. Each echo of abandonment was met with a whisper of compassion, each note of the shadow's song, with a melody of love. In the realm of the shadow, coping isn't a battle but a dance. It's a dance where acknowledgment, expression, and self-compassion are the steps. Each step is a movement towards wholeness, each dance, a journey into the sanctuaries of the soul. In this dance, the shadow isn't an adversary but a partner. It unveils not to confront but to connect, not to isolate but to integrate. In the dance of coping, we don't just encounter the whispers of the shadow but the melodies of our soul, in all its intricate, enigmatic, and beautiful symphony. Each note, a step towards wholeness; each dance, a journey into the sanctuaries of the complete, unfiltered, and beautiful self.

Reflecting Questions

Reflect on a moment when an unexpected emotion or reaction surfaced within you. What insights can this instance provide about the hidden aspects of your shadow self?

_____

_____

_____

_____

As you consider the practical tools and strategies discussed, which one resonates with you the most, and how might implementing it deepen your understanding of your shadow?

_____

_____

_____

_____

Recall a real-life scenario where you noticed the emergence of your shadow. How did it manifest, and what did this revelation teach you about your inner self?

_____

_____

_____

_____

The Benefits of Shadow Work

Embarking on the journey of shadow work is akin to stepping into a garden that has been left untended. Amidst the overgrown weeds and untamed branches, there lies the potential for blossoming flowers and thriving greenery. It is a journey of unearthing, nurturing, and witnessing the blossoming of the self, a transformative process that unveils not just the concealed aspects of our identity but illuminates the path to holistic well-being.

One of the most profound benefits of shadow work is the attainment of emotional freedom. Imagine being unshackled from the chains of suppressed emotions, where every concealed fear, muted anger, and unexpressed joy is given the space to breathe, to exist, and to transform. This liberation is not just an emotional unburdening but a gateway to a heightened sense of self-awareness, where the self is not fragmented but whole, not concealed but revealed. In this unveiling, there is an enhanced clarity of thought. The fog of confusion, doubt, and uncertainty begins to dissipate. Decisions are no longer a battle but a harmonious process, where intuition and logic dance in unison. The inner voice, often muted amidst the noise of external influences and internal conflicts, finds its tone, its resonance, and its expression.

Shadow work also paves the path to enriched relationships. When the self is understood, acknowledged, and embraced in its entirety, the external reflections of these internal dynamics begin to transform. Relationships cease to be a space of projection, where the concealed shadows find inadvertent and often, unconscious expressions. Instead, they become a space of authentic interactions, where understanding, empathy, and connection flourish. The journey inward also illuminates the paths of creativity. In the recesses of the shadow self, lie unexpressed ideas, muted expressions, and untapped potentials. As the shadow is acknowledged, the dams holding back the rivers of creativity begin to crumble. Ideas flow with an unbridled vigor, expressions find their unfiltered voice, and potentials begin to manifest in tangible realities.

In the garden of the self, where the light of consciousness illuminates the shadows, there is a blossoming of inner peace. It's a tranquility that is not contingent on external validations or material acquisitions but is rooted in the profound acceptance of the self, in all its shades, nuances, and intricacies. It's a peace that is not a destination but a journey, where every step, every acknowledgment, and every unveiling is a dance of harmony, a symphony of existence.

As the journey of shadow work unfolds, the garden of the self, once untended, begins to thrive. The weeds of suppressed emotions, unexpressed potentials, and concealed aspects are transformed. In their place, flowers of emotional freedom, clarity, enriched relationships, unbridled creativity, and inner peace blossom. Each flower a testament to the transformative, illuminating, and liberating journey of shadow work, where the self is not just discovered but celebrated, not just acknowledged but embraced, in all its profound, intricate, and beautiful existence.

Stories of Unveiling

Emma, a therapist by profession, had always prided herself on her ability to navigate the emotional landscapes of others. Yet, there was a silent storm brewing within her, a tempest of emotions and aspects of herself that remained unexplored. The journey of shadow work for Emma was not a choice but a calling, an undeniable pull towards the depths of her inner world.

"I found parts of myself I didn't know existed," Emma recalls. "There were emotions, reactions, and even desires that I had neatly tucked away, believing they had no place in the composed narrative of my life. Shadow work was like walking into a room within myself that I had locked away." The unlocking of this room was not just a revelation but a transformation. Emma speaks of an emotional fluidity, a grace in navigating not just the joys but the storms. "It's like the emotional walls I had built, the rigid boundaries, they all dissolved. I could feel deeply, wholly, without the fear of being consumed by my emotions."

For Alex, a corporate executive, the journey into the shadow was initiated by a crisis. A career that seemed fulfilling, relationships that appeared harmonious, yet a void, an inexplicable emptiness that echoed within. "I was successful, but not fulfilled. Connected, yet lonely. It was a paradox I couldn't unravel until I stepped into the shadow," Alex shares.

The journey for Alex was akin to weaving through a labyrinth, where each turn, each twist, unveiled a hidden aspect of the self. "I realized I had worn masks, so many of them, that I had lost sight of my authentic self. In the corridors of the shadow, each mask fell away, and I was face to face with a self that was raw, real, and radiant." The unmasking brought with it a liberation. Alex's relationships transformed, the void was filled, not with achievements or acquisitions but with an authentic connection to the self. "I was no longer playing roles. I was living my truth. In meetings, in relationships, there was an authenticity, a transparency that was liberating."

For Maya, an artist, the shadow was a silent muse. It was a space where unexpressed ideas, muted creativity, and stifled expressions found a voice. "My art was appreciated, but it wasn't alive. It was a reflection of the masks I wore, not the soul that longed to express," Maya reflects. The canvases began to change as Maya delved into the shadow. Each stroke of the brush was infused with the echoes of the unexpressed, each creation, a dance of the concealed and the conscious. "My art became a journey, each creation, a step towards the self. It was alive, pulsating with the rhythms of the soul that was no longer in the shadows."

Emma, Alex, and Maya, distinct journeys, yet united by the transformative power of shadow work. It's a testament to the liberation, authenticity, and aliveness that awaits in the depths of the shadow. A world where emotions flow with grace, where masks fall away to unveil the authentic self, where creativity is not a process but a living, breathing entity. In the echoes of their journeys, the silent song of the shadow finds its voice, a melody of transformation, liberation, and authentic existence.

The Evolving Benefits of Shadow Work

In the silent, yet profound journey of shadow work, the transformations and revelations are not static but dynamic, not finite but infinite. They are akin to the blossoming of a flower that unveils its petals one by one, each unveiling revealing a new layer of beauty, a new depth of essence.

Emma, who once found emotional fluidity in the initial phases of her shadow work, discovered something even more profound as time unfolded. "It wasn't just about feeling deeply," she reflects. "It was about a wisdom that was rooted, not in learned knowledge, but in lived experiences. Every emotion, every unveiling of the shadow, became a stepping stone to a wisdom that was intuitive, innate." This wisdom was not confined to the self but extended its gentle tendrils into her professional life, transforming her interactions with her clients. Each session became a dance of depth, where empathy was not a tool but an authentic experience, where healing was not a process but a joint journey into the depths of the human experience. For Alex, the unmasking of the self in the corporate corridors and personal relationships evolved into a leadership that was not about authority but authenticity. "I was no longer leading teams; I was part of a collective journey. Every project, every assignment was a dance of diverse, yet united souls," Alex shares. This leadership was not about directives but about dialogues, not about authority but about authentic connections. The corporate corridors, once a space of masked identities and concealed potentials, transformed into arenas of innovation, creativity, and collective progress.

Maya's dance with the shadow, which breathed life into her art, evolved into a creativity that was not confined to the canvas but spilled into every aspect of her life. "Every interaction became a canvas, every experience, a stroke of the brush. Life was no longer a series of events but a living, breathing masterpiece of the soul's silent songs," Maya reflects. This creativity was not a solitary journey but a collective dance. Every creation, every expression became a bridge, connecting souls, unveiling the universal echoes of the human experience, transcending boundaries of language, culture, and identities. The journey of shadow work is not a chapter but a book, not a song but a symphony. It's a dance where every step unveils a new movement, every note reveals a new melody.

Emma's emotional fluidity blossomed into intuitive wisdom; Alex's authentic existence transformed into authentic leadership; Maya's living art evolved into a living masterpiece of existence. In the evolving benefits of shadow work, we find the echoes of a journey that is not linear but circular, not finite but infinite. It's a dance of the soul where every step is a revelation, every movement, a transformation. In this dance, the shadow is not a silent spectator but an active participant, unveiling, with every step, the infinite, profound, and beautiful symphony of our existence.

Reflecting Questions

How do the positive outcomes of shadow work, such as emotional freedom and enhanced self-awareness, resonate with your personal journey of self-discovery and growth?

_____

_____

_____

_____

Reflecting on the testimonials shared, in what ways can you relate to the transformations experienced by Emma, Alex, and Maya in your own process of embracing the shadow self?

_____

_____

_____

_____

As you consider the evolving benefits of shadow work over time, what aspirations or hopes do you hold for your own continuous journey of inner exploration and transformation?

_____

_____

_____

_____

Carl Jung's Four Main Archetypes

In the intricate tapestry of the human psyche, woven with threads of conscious thoughts and unconscious echoes, Carl Jung identified four primary archetypes that reside within us all. These archetypes, universal and foundational, are not mere concepts but living entities that breathe life into our thoughts, actions, and interactions.

The first of these is the Self, the core, the center of the psychological universe around which all other aspects revolve. It is the unifying force, the harmonizer of the conscious and unconscious realms of our existence. The Self is not static but dynamic, an evolving entity that seeks integration and wholeness. It is the archetype that embarks on the heroic journey of self-discovery, confronting, and embracing the multifaceted dimensions of the human experience.

Then there is the Anima or Animus, the feminine and masculine energies that reside within us, irrespective of our gender. The Anima, the feminine within, is the nurturer, the wellspring of compassion, intuition, and emotionality. She is the bridge to the unconscious, the mediator who unveils the hidden realms of the psyche. The Animus, the masculine within, is the voice of reason, logic, and assertiveness. He is the warrior and the sage, embodying strength and wisdom.

The third archetype, the Persona, is the mask, the social self that we present to the world. It is the adaptive entity, crafted and refined by societal norms, expectations, and roles. The Persona is not the authentic self but the role we play, the mask we wear, a necessary adaptation to navigate the social terrains of our existence. It is both a shield and a mediator, protecting the vulnerable inner world while facilitating our interactions in the external world.

Last, but by no means least, is the Shadow, the concealed, the denied, the repressed. It is the reservoir of aspects that the conscious self refuses to acknowledge. The Shadow is not merely the dark or negative but encompasses all that is unexpressed, including latent talents and positive attributes. It is the echo of the un-lived life, the whisper of the unexpressed self, residing in the silent corridors of the unconscious.

Each archetype, distinct yet interconnected, contributes to the complex, multifaceted narrative of our existence. They are not isolated entities but integral aspects of our being, each breathing life into our thoughts, actions, and interactions. In the dance of these archetypes, in their silent songs and expressive echoes, we find the intricate, enigmatic, and beautiful symphony of the human psyche. Each note, each echo, is a step towards understanding the profound, intricate narrative of not just who we are, but who we have the potential to become.

Choreography of Consciousness

As if stepping into a grand theatre where the curtains draw back to reveal a complex dance of characters, each reader is invited to witness the dynamic interplay of Carl Jung's four primary archetypes. Imagine each archetype as a dancer, moving with grace, each step, each motion echoing the silent songs of the psyche. They don't dance in isolation but in unison, weaving a narrative that is as complex as it is beautiful.

The Self, the core dancer, moves with an aura of integration, drawing the others into a harmonious ballet. It's a dance of unity, where the Self seeks to weave the distinct steps and motions of the other archetypes into a seamless performance.

Enter the Anima and Animus, the dancers representing the feminine and masculine energies within us. They move with grace and precision, their steps echoing the intuitive and rational, the nurturing and assertive. They are the bridges, connecting the conscious applause of the audience with the unconscious echoes of the backstage, where emotions and thoughts reside in silent anticipation.

The Persona, a dancer wearing masks, adapts its performance to the audience's expectations. It's a dance of adaptation, where the masks are not barriers but bridges, facilitating the dancer's movement across the stage of life, echoing the societal norms and roles.

In the shadowy corners of the stage, the Shadow dancer moves with silent grace. It's not an interruption but a contribution, adding depth to the performance with its unexpressed emotions and concealed aspects. The Shadow is the echo of the un-lived dance, the silent steps that find their rhythm and motion in the grand performance of the psyche.

In this theatre, the dance is not scripted but spontaneous, not isolated but interconnected. The Self, Anima or Animus, Persona, and Shadow move with grace, each step a note in the silent symphony of the psyche. It's a performance where each note, each echo, is a revelation, an unveiling of the profound narrative of who we are and who we are becoming. Each step, each motion, is an invitation to witness, to explore, and to embrace the silent songs and expressive dances of the archetypes within us all.

Archetypes Illuminating the Shadow

As we delve deeper into the intricate dance of the archetypes, a realization dawns that this dance is not just a spectacle but a source of profound insights. Each archetype, with its unique movements and rhythms, illuminates corners of the shadow, unveiling aspects that are often concealed in the silent corridors of the unconscious.

The Self, with its integrative dance, brings a light of wholeness. It illuminates the fragmented pieces residing within the shadow, offering an opportunity for integration. It's a dance of unity, where the scattered pieces of the self are brought into the light, acknowledged, and embraced.

The dance of the Anima and Animus, with its harmonious blend of feminine and masculine energies, shines a light on the dualities residing within the shadow. It unveils the suppressed emotions, the unexpressed potentials, the silent echoes of the masculine and feminine that reside within the depths of each individual. It's a dance of balance, where the light and dark, the expressed and unexpressed, find a harmonious rhythm.

The Persona, with its adaptive dance, illuminates the roles and masks that often conceal the authentic self. It brings awareness to the adaptations, the compromises, the silent sacrifices that are often made to fit into societal norms and expectations. It's a dance of revelation, where the masks fall away to unveil the authentic rhythms of the self.

In this dance, the shadow is not a passive observer but an active participant. Each movement of the archetypes, each rhythm, each step, illuminates aspects of the shadow, bringing them into the light of conscious awareness. It's a dance of revelation, where the concealed emotions, the suppressed aspects, the latent potentials find expression and acknowledgment.

Understanding these archetypes is akin to holding a lantern in the intricate corridors of the shadow. Each archetype, with its unique light, illuminates aspects that are often concealed, offering an opportunity for acknowledgment, exploration, and integration. It's a journey of illumination, where the silent echoes of the shadow find a voice, where the concealed aspects are unveiled, and where the journey of integration and wholeness finds its rhythm and motion.

In the dance of the archetypes, the shadow is not a silent, concealed entity but a living, breathing aspect of the self. It is illuminated by the rhythms of the Self, the balance of the Anima and Animus, the revelations of the Persona. Each dance, each movement, is a step towards the illumination of the shadow, offering an opportunity for exploration, acknowledgment, and integration in the profound journey of self-discovery and wholeness.

Reflecting Questions

How do you perceive the dance between your inner archetypes - the Self, Anima or Animus, Persona, and Shadow - influencing your thoughts, emotions, and actions in daily life?

_____

_____

_____

_____

_____

In what ways have you experienced the adaptive dance of the Persona, and how has it impacted your authentic self and the shadows that remain unilluminated?

_____

_____

_____

_____

Reflect on the balance between your Anima and Animus. How do these feminine and masculine energies within you reveal themselves, and what shadows might they be casting or illuminating?

_____

_____

_____

_____

Considering the interplay of the archetypes, how might a deeper understanding of each contribute to unveiling and integrating the concealed aspects of your Shadow, enhancing your journey to self-discovery and wholeness?

_____

_____

_____

_____

Understanding How Your Shadow Works

Imagine for a moment, a vast, intricate machine, hidden in the depths of a grand, ancient castle. This machine, with its gears and levers, pulleys and pendulums, is as enigmatic as it is powerful. It hums silently, echoing the rhythms of a concealed world, a world where the shadow resides, operates, and influences.

The shadow, though often silent and unseen, is not passive. It is a dynamic entity, a living, breathing mechanism that operates with precision, influenced by the intricate dance of the archetypes, the silent echoes of the unconscious, and the loud narratives of the conscious world. It's a mechanism of defense and protection, where the shadow, with its concealed emotions and unexpressed potentials, acts as a guardian of the psyche. It holds within its silent corridors, the emotions, desires, and aspects that are too potent, too raw, to be faced in the light of conscious awareness. It's a sanctuary and a prison, a guardian and a gatekeeper. Yet, the shadow is also a mechanism of expression. It finds its voice in the silent echoes of our dreams, the unscripted moments of our reactions, the unguarded instances of our expressions. It's not a silent observer but an active participant, echoing the unexpressed, the concealed, the denied, in the loud theatre of our conscious world. The shadow operates with a logic of its own, a logic that is not linear but circular, not explicit but implicit. It's a dance of concealment and revelation, where the shadow hides yet seeks expression, conceals yet reveals, denies yet affirms. In the silent machinery of the shadow, there is a wisdom, a profound intelligence that seeks not just to conceal but to integrate. Each emotion, each desire, each aspect held within the silent corridors of the shadow, seeks not just concealment but acknowledgment, not just sanctuary but expression.

As we delve deeper into the hidden machinery of the shadow, a realization dawns. The shadow is not an antagonist but a companion, not a prison but a sanctuary, not a denial but an affirmation. It's a living, breathing mechanism that operates with a wisdom, a precision, echoing the rhythms of a world that is as enigmatic as it is profound. In the silent hum of this machinery, in the concealed corridors of this ancient, grand castle, lies an invitation. An invitation to explore, to understand, to integrate. It's a journey into the depths, where the silent songs of the shadow echo with a wisdom, a revelation, unveiling the concealed, the denied, the unexpressed, in the loud, intricate dance of our conscious existence.

The Psychological Landscape

In the enigmatic dance of consciousness, where light and shadow intertwine, there lies a psychological landscape, vast and intricate. It is a terrain shaped by the silent echoes of the unconscious, the loud narratives of the conscious, and the uncharted territories where they meet. Here, in this complex terrain, the mechanisms of the shadow weave their silent yet profound narratives.

The shadow is not a static entity but a dynamic force, shaped by the psychological processes that are as complex as they are profound. It is influenced by the repressed emotions, the unacknowledged desires, the silent fears, and the unexpressed potentials that reside in the silent corridors of the unconscious. Yet, the shadow is not a silent prisoner of the unconscious but a bridge, a gateway where the silent echoes of the unconscious meet the loud narratives of the conscious. It is shaped by the defense mechanisms, the cognitive processes, the emotional responses that are enacted in the loud theatre of our conscious existence.

In this psychological landscape, repression plays a pivotal role. It is the silent guardian that conceals the potent, raw emotions and desires in the silent corridors of the unconscious. Yet, repression is not a jailer but a guardian, protecting the conscious self from the overwhelming torrents of unprocessed emotions and desires.

Projection is another silent actor in this intricate dance. It is the mechanism where the shadow, with its concealed aspects, finds expression in the outer world. The unacknowledged emotions, the unexpressed desires, are projected onto the world, echoing the silent narratives of the shadow in the loud theatre of existence.

Yet, in this complex terrain, there is also the dance of integration. The shadow, though concealed, seeks acknowledgment. It is a dance where the repressed emotions, the unacknowledged desires, seek light, expression, and integration. It is a journey from the silent corridors of repression to the loud narratives of expression, from the concealed territories of the unconscious to the acknowledged landscapes of the conscious.

In this psychological landscape, the shadow is not a passive entity but an active force. It is shaped by the silent echoes of repression, the loud narratives of projection, the uncharted territories of integration. It is a dance of concealment and revelation, where the shadow, with its concealed aspects, seeks not just sanctuary but expression, not just concealment but acknowledgment. As we navigate this complex terrain, a realization dawns. The shadow is not an antagonist but a companion, not a prison but a sanctuary, not a denial but an affirmation. It is a living, breathing entity that echoes the silent songs and loud narratives of a psychological landscape that is as enigmatic as it is profound.

Navigating the Shadow's Mechanisms

In the intricate dance between light and shadow, a path unfolds, inviting us on a journey of exploration and integration. The shadow, with its concealed corridors and silent echoes, is not a territory to be feared but to be understood, not a landscape to be avoided but to be navigated. The mechanisms of the shadow, intricate and profound, offer insights that are as illuminating as they are transformative. Each mechanism, each process, is a map, a guide, echoing the pathways that lead to the concealed territories of the self.

Understanding the shadow's mechanisms is akin to holding a lantern in a grand, ancient castle. Each corridor, each pathway, illuminated by the light of understanding, unveils aspects that are often concealed, offering an opportunity for acknowledgment, exploration, and integration. Yet, this is not a journey of conquest but of companionship, not of domination but of dialogue. The shadow, with its concealed emotions and unexpressed potentials, seeks not suppression but acknowledgment, not avoidance but engagement.

In this journey, curiosity is the compass. It is a curiosity that is gentle yet profound, silent yet illuminating. It is a curiosity that seeks to understand, to explore, to unveil. Each question, each inquiry, is a step, a movement, echoing the pathways that lead to the concealed, the denied, the unexpressed.

Patience, too, is a silent companion on this journey. The shadow, with its intricate mechanisms and concealed corridors, unveils its secrets not in haste but in silence, not in noise but in whispers. Each insight, each revelation, is a silent song, echoing the rhythms of a dance that is as enigmatic as it is profound.

Yet, in this journey, there is also the dance of compassion. The shadow, with its concealed emotions and unexpressed potentials, is not a territory of judgment but of understanding, not of criticism but of compassion. Each emotion, each desire, each aspect held within the silent corridors of the shadow, seeks not judgment but understanding, not criticism but compassion.

As we navigate the intricate mechanisms of the shadow, a realization dawns. This is not a journey of isolation but of companionship, not of avoidance but of engagement, not of suppression but of expression. In the silent echoes and loud narratives of the shadow's mechanisms, lies an invitation - an invitation to a dance that is as illuminating as it is transformative, as enigmatic as it is profound.

Reflecting Questions

How do you perceive the mechanisms of your own shadow, and in what ways have you noticed them influencing your thoughts, emotions, and behaviors?

_____

_____

_____

_____

_____

Reflect on a moment where repression or projection was evident in your reactions or behaviors. How did these psychological processes shape your experience and interactions with others?

_____

_____

_____

_____

As you consider the dance of integration, what insights or realizations have emerged about the concealed aspects of your shadow seeking acknowledgment and expression?

_____

_____

_____

_____

How can curiosity and compassion serve as tools in your journey of navigating and understanding the intricate mechanisms of your shadow, leading to personal growth and self-discovery?

_____

_____

_____

_____

Disarming the Inner Critic

Every individual, at various points in their life, encounters a voice that is less than kind. It's a voice that casts doubt, incites anxiety, and fosters a sense of inadequacy. This voice, known as the inner critic, is not a fleeting whisper but a persistent echo, often shaping our self-perception and interactions with the world.

The origins of the inner critic are as varied as they are complex. It is a construct, a synthesis of external voices of judgment and expectation that have been internalized over the years. Parents, teachers, peers, media, and society at large contribute to this narrative. Each criticism, whether explicit or implicit, each expectation, whether reasonable or unattainable, weaves itself into the fabric of our psyche. Over time, these external voices become internalized, giving birth to the inner critic. Yet, this critic is not a monolithic entity. It is multifaceted, echoing the diverse sources from which it draws its narrative. It speaks the language of 'shoulds' and 'musts', echoing a script that is as rigid as it is exacting. It is a voice that can be as harsh as it is persistent, casting shadows of doubt, anxiety, and inadequacy. However, the inner critic, though formidable, is not invincible. It is a construct, and like all constructs, it can be deconstructed and understood. It is not an absolute authority but a relative narrative, shaped by the dynamics of internalized judgments and expectations.

The journey to confront and understand the inner critic is an exploration into the depths of the self. It is a journey that requires courage, for it involves facing not just the critic but the silent fears, unspoken insecurities, and concealed vulnerabilities that it echoes. It is a journey of unmasking, where the rigid narratives of 'shoulds' and 'musts' are unveiled, examined, and understood. This journey is also one of transformation. For in confronting the inner critic, we are not just facing a voice of judgment but unearthing the hidden corridors of the self. Each criticism, each judgment, each expectation echoed by the inner critic is a doorway, an entry point into the concealed landscapes of our psyche.

In this exploration, insights emerge. The inner critic, though harsh, is not without purpose. It is a protector, albeit misguided, seeking to shield the self from the perceived dangers of judgment, failure, and rejection. It is a guardian, albeit overzealous, echoing the silent fears and unspoken insecurities that reside within the hidden recesses of the self.

Yet, in its protection lies its paradox. For the inner critic, in its zeal to protect, often stifles. It silences the voice of authenticity, dims the light of potential, and casts shadows of doubt and inadequacy. It is a voice that, in its quest to shield, often imprisons, turning the rich landscapes of the self into silent corridors of concealment. Confronting the inner critic is, therefore, a liberation. It is an unmasking of the silent fears, unspoken insecurities, and concealed vulnerabilities that it echoes. It is a dialogue, where the rigid narratives of 'shoulds' and 'musts' are not just heard but understood, not just echoed but transformed.

In this dialogue, a transformation unfolds. The inner critic, though persistent, is not immutable. In the light of understanding, its rigid narratives soften, its harsh judgments dissipate, and its exacting expectations transform. It becomes not a voice of constraint but a dialogue of liberation, echoing the silent song of a self that is as diverse as it is dynamic, as potential as it is profound.

Strategies to Silence the Inner Critic

The inner critic, with its persistent and often harsh narrative, can be a formidable adversary. However, it is not invincible. There are specific strategies that can be employed to not only silence this internal voice but transform it into a source of empowerment and self-compassion. The first step is recognition. The inner critic often operates in the background, its narrative so ingrained that it becomes an almost unconscious reflex. Bringing this voice into the conscious realm, acknowledging its presence, and identifying its triggers is essential. It's about listening intently, not to succumb but to understand, not to internalize but to analyze.

Journaling can be a powerful tool in this phase. Writing down the critical thoughts as they arise, capturing the specific words and phrases the inner critic employs, can bring clarity. It externalizes the internal narrative, providing a platform for reflection and analysis. Once recognized, the next step is to challenge the inner critic. It's about questioning the validity of its claims, evaluating the evidence, and distinguishing between objective reality and subjective interpretation. This process of inquiry can unveil the distortions, generalizations, and black-and-white thinking that often characterize the inner critic's narrative.

A helpful strategy here is to adopt the role of a compassionate observer. Imagine a friend or loved one expressing the same critical thoughts about themselves. What would be your response? This shift in perspective can foster empathy and compassion, illuminating the harshness of the inner critic and opening pathways for a more balanced and compassionate narrative. The third step is to reframe. The inner critic is not just a voice of judgment but a reflection of underlying beliefs and assumptions. Identifying these core beliefs, examining their origins, and assessing their validity is crucial. It's about delving beneath the surface narrative to uncover the foundational beliefs that fuel the inner critic. Reframing involves crafting an alternative narrative, one that is balanced, compassionate, and empowering. It's about replacing the rigid 'shoulds' and 'musts' with flexible preferences, the absolute judgments with nuanced assessments, the categorical imperatives with compassionate inclinations.

Visualization can be a potent ally in this phase. Envisioning a scenario where the critical thoughts are replaced with empowering narratives, imagining the feelings, responses, and behaviors this new narrative elicits, can reinforce the reframing process. It's about not just conceptualizing but experiencing the alternative narrative, integrating it into the emotional and behavioral repertoire.

The final step is to cultivate self-compassion. The inner critic thrives on perfectionism, on the relentless pursuit of unattainable standards. Self-compassion involves acknowledging our inherent human imperfection, embracing our flaws and vulnerabilities with kindness and understanding. Mindfulness practices can nurture this compassionate stance. Through meditation and focused attention, we can learn to observe our thoughts and feelings without judgment, to sit with our imperfections without condemnation, to embrace our vulnerabilities without shame. In silencing the inner critic, the transformation is profound. The rigid narratives loosen, the harsh judgments soften, and the exacting expectations transform. We step into a space of self-compassion, empowerment, and authenticity, where the silent song of the self emerges, not in the echoes of judgment but in the melodies of compassion, not in the shadows of inadequacy but in the light of inherent worth.

The Transformation Unleashed

When the inner critic is disarmed, a profound transformation occurs. It's akin to stepping out from a perpetual shadow into the light, where the self is no longer a battlefield of harsh judgments and unattainable expectations but a sanctuary of compassion, acceptance, and empowerment.

This transformation is not an abstract concept; it's tangible and experiential. It's felt in the quiet moments when self-judgment is replaced by self-compassion, where the rigid 'shoulds' and 'musts' give way to preferences and inclinations that honor the self's authenticity. In the absence of the inner critic's persistent narrative, a silence emerges. But it's not the silence of absence; it's the silence of presence. It's in this silence that the whispers of the authentic self become audible. These are not the echoes of judgment but the melodies of inherent worth, not the refrains of inadequacy but the harmonies of innate potential.

Life takes on a different hue. The external world, once a mirror reflecting the inner critic's harsh judgments, transforms into a canvas, a space of exploration, expression, and expansion. Relationships, once arenas of performance and perfection, become sanctuaries of connection and authenticity. The disarming of the inner critic is not the eradication of self-evaluation. Instead, it's a transformation of the evaluative lens. Assessment and reflection, once tinted with the harsh hues of judgment, are now colored with the soft tones of compassion and understanding. Mistakes and imperfections, once sources of shame and concealment, become opportunities for growth and self-discovery.

In this transformed space, the self is no longer a static entity defined by rigid narratives but a dynamic being, evolving, and unfolding. Each moment, each experience, is not a test of worth but an opportunity for self-expression, not an evaluation of adequacy but a celebration of authenticity. The inner dialogue transforms. The voice of the inner critic, once loud and persistent, recedes, and in its place, a new narrative emerges. It's a narrative that speaks the language of 'I am enough', that echoes the refrains of inherent worth, that sings the melodies of unconditional self-acceptance. This transformation is not a destination but a journey, not an attainment but a process. It's a journey of returning, again and again, to the sanctuary of the self, where worth is not earned but inherent, where acceptance is not conditional but unconditional, where the self is not an object of judgment but a subject of compassion.

Reflecting Questions

How has your inner critic shaped your self-perception and influenced your actions? Reflect on specific instances where you felt its presence.

_____

_____

_____

_____

Consider the strategies mentioned for disarming the inner critic. Which of these resonate with you the most, and how might they transform your relationship with yourself?

_____

_____

_____

_____

Imagine a day without the influence of your inner critic. How would this freedom from self-judgment impact your emotions, thoughts, and actions?

_____

_____

_____

Connecting with Your Inner Child

The inner child, a concept deeply rooted in psychological paradigms, is not a novel entity but an integral part of our psyche that encapsulates the innocence, wonder, and traumas of our formative years. It's a reservoir of both the joyous laughter that echoed in our childhood playgrounds and the silent tears that were never seen, a blend of the playful and the pained, the cherished and the chagrined.

This inner child is not a metaphorical construct but a palpable force that breathes life into our adult selves. It shapes our reactions, molds our fears, and crafts our desires. It is the silent whisper behind our joys and the shadowy echo behind our sorrows. It is as real as the skin that wraps our bones and as tangible as the breath that fills our lungs.

Every unexplained fear, every inexplicable joy, every emotion that seems to emerge from the abyss of the unknown, is often a melody sung by the inner child. It is a song composed in the years when the world was a canvas of wonder, a time when joy was unbridled, and pain, though often silent, was as piercing as the winter's cold.

Yet, in the hustle of adulting, amidst the noise of responsibilities and the clamor of societal expectations, the voice of the inner child often becomes a faint echo, unheard, unacknowledged. We march forward, armored with the sophistication of adulthood, yet, unknowingly, we carry the silent child within, with its unuttered words and unexpressed emotions.

The impacts of this inner entity are profound. It is the silent architect crafting the corridors of our emotional world. The joys that inexplicably elevate our spirits are often the echoes of the child's laughter, and the fears that inexplicably chain our souls are the silent screams of the child unseen, unheard.

Acknowledging this inner child is not an act of regression but a journey of progression. It's not about returning to childhood but about honoring the child within, listening to its silent songs, hearing its unspoken words, feeling its unfelt emotions. It's a journey of giving voice to the silent screams and ears to the unuttered words.

In the silent spaces of this acknowledgment, healing begins. The adult self, armored with the wisdom of years, and the child self, endowed with the innocence of youth, meet. In this meeting, the fragmented pieces of the self begin to merge, the scattered notes of our song begin to harmonize, and the disjoined steps of our dance begin to synchronize.

We are not just beings of the present, armored with the wisdom and wounds of the years. We are echoes of a past, carriers of a child, holders of a history. In the silent spaces of our souls, amidst the noise of our thoughts and the clamor of our emotions, the inner child waits - silent yet speaking, invisible yet present, echoing the songs of a past that breathes life into our present.

Embracing the Inner Child

The journey to connect with the inner child is a dance between the past and present, a harmonious ballet that weaves the threads of yesteryears into the tapestry of today. It's not a descent into bygone days but an ascent into a realm where the echoes of the child's laughter and cries still linger, shaping, molding, and coloring the adult's world.

One of the most profound steps in this dance is the act of listening. The inner child, though silent, speaks the language of emotions, a dialect rich in hues, tones, and textures. Every unexplained joy, every inexplicable fear is a word in this child's lexicon, a note in its melody, a step in its dance.

A simple yet profound exercise to initiate this dialogue is the practice of silent sitting. In the quietude of silence, away from the noise of the world and the clamor of the mind, the whispers of the inner child become audible. It's a space where the adult self is not a speaker but a listener, not a teacher but a student, not a guide but a follower.

In this silence, we ask not the questions of the mind but the inquiries of the soul. "What joys of yesteryears still linger in the corridors of my soul? What pains of the past still echo in the chambers of my heart?" These are not questions seeking answers but inquiries inviting feelings, emotions, and sensations.

Another profound step in this dance is the act of expression. The inner child, though eloquent, often speaks a language that transcends words. It's a dialect of colors, shapes, and forms. The canvas, not the diary, is often the space where this child's words unfold, where its stories are told, where its emotions unfold.

A practice of uninhibited painting, where the brush is not guided by the skill of the hand but the impulses of the soul, becomes a bridge connecting the adult to the child. It's a space where colors tell stories, shapes narrate tales, and forms express emotions. It's a narrative where the canvas is a playground, and each stroke is a dance of the inner child.

Yet another step in this ballet is the act of play. The inner child is not a being of words but a soul of play, a spirit of joy. Revisiting the playgrounds of childhood, not with the sophistication of adulthood but the innocence of childhood, becomes a portal into the world of the inner child.

Engaging in the games of yesteryears, immersing in the plays of the past, not as an observer but a participant, not as a guide but a player, we enter the world of the inner child. It's a realm where play is not an act but a language, not a doing but a being, not a performance but an expression.

In this dance of listening, expressing, and playing, the adult and the child meet, not as strangers but as companions, not as two but as one. In this meeting, the silent songs of the inner child find voice, and the unheard melodies of yesteryears echo in the symphony of today.

The Healing Embrace

A transformation occurs when the inner child is not just seen but truly acknowledged. It's akin to the blossoming of a flower that has been in perpetual slumber, a silent symphony that finally finds its melody. The connection with the inner child isn't a mere acknowledgment of past pains and joys; it's a profound embrace of an integral part of the self that has been, until now, silently waiting in the wings.

The healing doesn't occur in the grand gestures but in the subtle, almost imperceptible moments of acknowledgment. It's in the silent nod to the child's fears, the gentle embrace of its pains, and the joyful celebration of its uninhibited laughter. This isn't a journey of fixing or mending but a graceful dance of accepting and being.

When the adult self takes the hand of the inner child, not with an intention to lead but to be led, a magical dance ensues. It's a dance where the wisdom of the adult and the innocence of the child are not at odds but in harmony, not in conflict but in concert. In this dance, the adult doesn't bring the healing; it becomes the healing.

The scars of the past begin to fade not when they are analyzed but when they are touched with the gentle hands of compassion. The wounds begin to mend not when they are understood but when they are held in the warm embrace of acceptance. The healing is not an act but a presence, not a doing but a being.

In this embrace, the adult self discovers a strength it never knew it had, and the inner child finds a voice it never knew it possessed. It's a meeting where silence speaks louder than words, and presence is more eloquent than speeches. In this space, the fragmented pieces of the self begin to converge into a harmonious whole.

The fears that once lurked in the dark corners of the soul begin to step into the light, not as formidable giants but as vulnerable children. The joys that were once imprisoned in the recesses of the heart begin to dance in the open fields of consciousness, not as fleeting moments but as eternal flames.

In this dance, the adult and the child are not two separate entities but two integral aspects of a single, harmonious self. The healing is not a journey from pain to pleasure, from wound to recovery, but a graceful dance from fragmentation to wholeness, from disconnection to unity, from silence to song.

In this space, every tear is a gem of wisdom, every laughter a song of freedom, every fear a step towards courage, and every joy a dance of the soul. The healing is not a destination but a journey, not an attainment but a becoming, not a possession but a presence.

In the gentle embrace of the inner child, the adult self doesn't just find the wounds of the past but the seeds of a future, not just the pains of yesteryears but the joys of tomorrows, not just the silence of the child but the song of the soul. In this embrace, we are not just healed; we are reborn.

Reflecting Questions

How does the concept of the inner child resonate with your personal experiences, and what emotions or memories emerge when you focus on this aspect of yourself?

_____

_____

_____

Reflecting on the exercises provided for connecting with the inner child, which ones elicited a strong response, and what insights did you gain about your hidden pains or unexpressed joys?

_____

_____

_____

As you consider the role of connecting with the inner child in the healing process, how do you envision this relationship evolving and enhancing your journey towards wholeness and self-discovery?

_____

_____

_____

Transforming Anger and Shame

Anger and shame are two powerful emotions, often rooted deeply within our psyche, their origins tracing back to intricate mazes of past experiences and learned behaviors. These emotions, though distinct, are intertwined in the complex dance of the human emotional spectrum. They are not just fleeting feelings but are often anchored in the profound depths of our subconscious, influencing our actions, reactions, and interactions.

Anger, a fiery, potent force, can be traced back to instances of injustice, violation, or threat. It is a natural, adaptive response to violations and serves as a signal that action is needed. Yet, when not understood or managed, anger can become destructive, leading to a cycle of regret, reconciliation, and recurrence.

Shame, on the other hand, is quieter but equally insidious. It whispers of inadequacy, unworthiness, and imperfection. It is born from a perception of self that is often distorted by critical evaluations, both internal and external. Shame is not just about what we've done but seeps into the core of who we believe we are, casting shadows of doubt and self-loathing.

These emotions, though uncomfortable, are not unnatural. They are part of the human experience, yet their power and intensity can be overwhelming. The roots of anger and shame often extend into childhood, where initial patterns of emotional response are formed. A child who experiences injustice or violation may develop a heightened sensitivity to such occurrences, their anger easily ignited. Similarly, a child exposed to constant criticism may internalize a sense of unworthiness, carrying the burden of shame into adulthood.

These emotions don't exist in isolation. They are often triggered by specific events, yet their intensity and impact are amplified by the underlying, unresolved issues that lurk in the shadows of the subconscious. The triggers are but the tip of the iceberg, visible manifestations of the profound, submerged emotional complexities.

Understanding the roots and manifestations of anger and shame is a journey into the self. It requires a willingness to peel back the layers, to venture into the uncomfortable spaces where pain, fear, and vulnerability reside. It is in these depths that transformation begins, where the fiery heat of anger and the icy grip of shame can be acknowledged, understood, and ultimately, transformed.

In this exploration, we are not seeking to eliminate these emotions. Anger has its place; it can be a catalyst for change, a signal that boundaries have been violated. Shame, too, in moderation, can serve as a reflection tool, a compass pointing towards areas of growth and development. The goal is not eradication but transformation, turning these potent forces into allies on the journey of self-discovery and healing.

Unleashing Transformation

In the journey of transforming anger and shame, the tools we employ are as intricate and profound as the emotions themselves. These aren't mere feelings but powerful forces that have shaped our identities, behaviors, and interactions. To transform them is to embark on a journey of self-discovery, a path that is as challenging as it is rewarding.

One of the first steps in this transformative journey is acknowledgment. Anger and shame thrive in the dark recesses of denial and suppression. Bringing them into the light, acknowledging their existence and their power, is the first step towards transformation. It's about giving ourselves the permission to feel, to experience these emotions in their raw, unfiltered intensity.

Journaling can be a potent tool in this phase of acknowledgment. Writing about the triggers, the feelings, and the underlying beliefs that fuel anger and shame can provide insights into their origins and patterns. It's a process of externalization, of taking the intangible turmoil of emotions and giving them shape, form, and substance on paper.

Visualization is another powerful strategy. It involves creating a mental image of these emotions, giving them shape, color, and form. In this tangible form, anger and shame become entities that can be observed, analyzed, and engaged with. Visualization transforms these emotions from overwhelming forces into manageable entities that can be interacted with, understood, and transformed.

Mindfulness and meditation are also integral in this journey. These practices anchor us in the present, creating a space where emotions can be experienced without judgment. In the silent spaces of meditation, the fiery heat of anger and the icy grip of shame are allowed to surface, to be felt and experienced in their entirety. It's a space of non-judgment, where these emotions are neither good nor bad; they simply are. Breathing exercises complement these practices, especially in moments of intense emotional upheaval. The breath becomes an anchor, a stabilizing force that grounds us in the present. In the midst of the stormy seas of anger and shame, the breath is a lighthouse, guiding us back to the shores of calm and stability. Transformation is not about suppression or elimination. It's about understanding, engagement, and integration. These tools are not weapons to vanquish anger and shame but instruments of illumination, shedding light on the dark corners where these emotions reside. In the light, transformation occurs, and from the ashes of anger and shame, a new, empowered self emerges, unburdened by the chains of the past and free to explore the limitless potentials of the future.

Embracing Acceptance and Compassion

The transformation of anger and shame is not a linear journey, but rather a dance between darkness and light, suppression and expression, pain and healing. It is a process that unfolds in the tender spaces of acceptance and compassion. These are not just emotional states but powerful catalysts that ignite the alchemy of transformation.

Acceptance is the silent acknowledgment that anger and shame exist within us. It is the gentle permission to allow these emotions to surface, to be seen, felt, and heard. Acceptance is not an endorsement of these emotions but a recognition of their existence. It is in this space of acknowledgment that the stifling grip of denial is loosened, and the healing light of awareness is allowed to penetrate the dark recesses where anger and shame reside.

Compassion is the warm embrace that surrounds these painful emotions. It is the tender touch that heals, the soft whisper that soothes, the gentle gaze that sees the pain and responds with love. Compassion is not just a feeling but an action, a dynamic force that transforms the rigid boundaries of anger and shame into the fluid contours of healing and integration.

In the crucible of acceptance and compassion, anger is not a demon to be slain but a messenger to be heard. It is a signal, a beacon illuminating the unmet needs, the unresolved conflicts, the suppressed pains that simmer beneath the surface. In the light of compassion, anger is allowed to speak, to unveil the stories of pain, injustice, and violation that have been silenced, ignored, and invalidated. Shame, too, finds a voice in this compassionate space. It is no longer a mark of unworthiness but a cry for love, acceptance, and belonging. In the tender embrace of compassion, shame is acknowledged, not as a testament to our inadequacy but as a reflection of our humanity, our vulnerability, our innate need for connection and affirmation.

In this journey, acceptance and compassion are not passive states but dynamic processes. They are practices that are cultivated, nurtured, and embodied. Every moment of acknowledgment, every act of compassion, is a step towards the transformation of anger and shame. It is a journey that unfolds in the silent spaces where judgment is suspended, and understanding is birthed, where the rigid narratives of blame, unworthiness, and victimhood are unraveled, giving way to the emerging stories of empowerment, worthiness, and healing. This is not a solitary journey but a communal dance. It is a process that is supported, facilitated, and enriched by the collective energies of community, connection, and mutual support. In this dance of transformation, every step taken, every insight gained, every breakthrough achieved, is not just a personal victory but a collective triumph, a testament to the indomitable power of the human spirit to transcend the shackles of pain and step into the limitless potentials of healing, wholeness, and integration.

Reflecting Questions

How have anger and shame manifested in your life, and what underlying unmet needs or unresolved conflicts might these emotions be signaling?

_____

_____

_____

_____

Reflect on a moment where acceptance and compassion played a significant role in alleviating the intensity of your anger or shame. How did this process unfold, and what insights did you gain about yourself?

_____

_____

_____

_____

In what ways can you cultivate a practice of acceptance and compassion to transform the narratives of blame, unworthiness, or victimhood associated with your anger and shame into stories of empowerment, worthiness, and healing?

_____

_____

_____

_____

Which tool for transforming anger and shame resonates with you, and how might you adapt it to your unique experience?

_____

_____

_____

_____

Part 2:
Exercises and Techniques for Shadow Work

Embarking on the journey of shadow work is akin to navigating an intricate labyrinth. The paths might seem confusing, and the turns unpredictable, but with the right tools and techniques, discovery awaits at every corner. In this significant second part, you will be equipped with a diverse arsenal of exercises and methodologies, each meticulously designed to help you delve deeper into your shadow self and the unconscious realms it resides in.

But why the variety? Because each individual resonates differently. While some might find solace and introspection through the tranquillity of mindfulness meditation, others may unearth profound realizations using the expressive freedom of creative art therapy. Our unique histories, experiences, and even traumas demand a multifaceted approach, and this part ensures there's something tailored for everyone.

Navigate through the calm introspection of guided imagery practices, the profound realizations that arise from narrative writing, or the cathartic release of role-playing scenarios. Each technique isn't just a mere activity but a gateway to deeper self-awareness, enabling you to confront, embrace, and ultimately integrate aspects of your shadow.

Moreover, this part recognizes the importance of holistic healing. Thus, you'll encounter methods that not only target the mind but also the body. From the rejuvenating experience of breathwork practices to the grounding calm of body scanning, the exercises appreciate the symbiotic relationship between the physical and mental.

Prepare to dive into a wellspring of self-discovery, as each chapter in this part holds a mirror to your inner world, reflects aspects you might have ignored, and paves the way for healing and integration. It's more than just understanding the shadow; it's about living the transformative process of shadow work daily.

Mindfulness Meditation Guide

Instructions:

Embark on a journey of inner exploration with this guided mindfulness meditation. Follow the steps below to immerse yourself in a moment of calm, awareness, and self-discovery.

Step 1: Find a quiet and comfortable space where you won't be disturbed. Sit or lie down in a relaxed position.

Step 2: Close your eyes gently and turn your attention inward. Begin to notice your breath. Feel the natural flow of air as you breathe in and out.

Step 3: As you breathe in, feel the air filling your lungs, and as you breathe out, imagine any tension or stress leaving your body.

Step 4: Your mind may wander, and thoughts or emotions may arise. Acknowledge them without judgment. Visualize them as clouds passing by in the sky, neither good nor bad, simply there.

Step 5: Each time your mind wanders, gently bring your focus back to your breath. Feel the rise and fall of your chest and the air moving in and out of your nostrils.

Step 6: Continue this process for 10-15 minutes. Allow yourself to be present, experiencing each breath, each thought, and each emotion with openness and curiosity.

Step 7: Gradually bring your awareness back to your surroundings. Wiggle your fingers and toes, and when you're ready, open your eyes.

Step 8: Sit quietly for a moment, acknowledging the peace and calm within you. Carry this sense of tranquility with you throughout your day.

Reflection Space:

Use the following space to record your experiences during the meditation. What thoughts and emotions arose? How did you feel before and after the meditation? There are no right or wrong answers, only your unique experience.

Date:

Thoughts and Emotions Observed:

_____

_____

_____

Physical Sensations Experienced:

_____

_____

_____

Insights Gained:

_____

_____

_____

_____

Overall Feelings:

_____

_____

_____

Creative Art Therapy Activities

Art possesses the profound power to give voice to the silent, hidden corridors of our subconscious. In this exercise, we'll harness the expressive capacities of art to explore and visualize the shadow self. Through drawing, painting, or collaging, you'll embark on a journey of self-discovery, unearthing emotions and aspects of yourself that often remain unspoken.

Below are art prompts designed to guide you in visually representing various facets of your shadow self, emotions, and specific experiences. Use the blank spaces provided to let your creativity flow freely. Remember, there's no right or wrong here; let intuition lead the way.

Colors of Emotion: Visualize an emotion you often struggle with. What colors, shapes, and images represent this emotion? Fill the space below with your visual representation.

The Hidden Self: Imagine your shadow self as a landscape. What does it look like? Is it a forest, a desert, an ocean, or something else? Create this landscape in the space below.

Emotional Release: Think of a specific experience that triggered strong emotions. Use colors and shapes to express these emotions and the experience in the space below.

Now take a moment to reflect on the process and the emotions that surfaced. Use the spaces below to jot down your feelings, insights, and any revelations about your shadow self that emerged during the art-making process.

Reflection on Prompt 1:

_____
_____
_____
_____

Reflection on Prompt 1:

_____
_____
_____
_____

Reflection on Prompt 1:

_____
_____
_____
_____

Narrative Writing Exercises

Narrative therapy is akin to being an author of your own life story. It's a process that allows you to explore, understand, and even rewrite the narratives that shape your identity, behaviors, and emotions. These narratives, often influenced by the shadow self, can either be empowering or limiting. In this exercise, you are given the pen to rewrite these stories, transforming them into sources of strength and self-discovery. Below are structured writing prompts designed to guide you in this intimate journey of exploring and rewriting the narratives about your identity, challenges, or past experiences. Remember, this is a sacred space of non-judgment and freedom, where every word you write is a step towards healing and self-discovery.

The Origin Story: *Write about a belief or narrative about yourself that you've held onto for years. Where did it originate? How has it shaped your life?*

_____

_____

_____

_____

The Turning Point: *Now, imagine a moment of transformation. Rewrite this narrative by focusing on strength, growth, and the lessons learned. How does this new story empower you?*

_____

_____

_____

_____

_____

_____

The Hero's Journey: *Identify a challenge you're currently facing. Write it out as a story, with you as the hero. What strengths and resources do you possess to overcome this challenge?*

_____

_____

_____

_____

_____

_____

The act of rewriting our narratives is not just about changing the words on a page; it's about transforming our internal world. In the spaces below, reflect on this process. Pay attention to any shifts in emotions, perspectives, and self-perception.

Emotional Landscape: *How did your emotions shift during this exercise? Were there moments of resistance, clarity, or release?*

_____

_____

_____

_____

_____

_____

A New Lens: *How has the process of rewriting your narrative influenced your perspective on the story and yourself?*

_____

_____

_____

_____

_____

The Unfolding Self: *In rewriting your narrative, what have you discovered about your inherent strengths and capabilities?*

_____

_____

_____

_____

_____

Guided Imagery Practice

Guided imagery is a powerful tool that invites us into a visual journey through the subconscious mind. It's a bridge to the unexplored terrains of the self, offering a safe space to encounter, converse, and integrate the shadow self. In this practice, you'll be led through a detailed script, a pathway, where imagery, emotions, and insights intertwine, offering a profound space for self-discovery and healing.

Practice

Close your eyes and take three deep breaths, allowing the inhales to fill you with calmness and the exhales to release tension. Visualize yourself in a serene forest, the sun gently piercing through the canopy, casting dancing shadows upon the forest floor.

As you walk, you notice a pathway veiled in soft shadows, inviting you yet filled with mystery. With each step, you feel a magnetic pull, a call to venture deeper. The rustling leaves and the gentle breeze whisper the ancient songs of self-discovery.

In the heart of the forest, you encounter a clearing where the light and shadows merge. Here, amidst the dance of light and dark, your shadow self emerges. It's a reflection of you, yet holds the aspects that have long been buried, unacknowledged, and unexpressed.

Engage in a dialogue. Ask your shadow self questions. What does it want you to know? What emotions and insights does it hold? Allow this conversation to unfold naturally, observing the emotions and insights that surface with compassion and curiosity.

As the dialogue deepens, visualize a merging of light and shadow, an integration where acceptance and understanding bloom. Feel the transformation, the wholeness that emerges from this union.

When you're ready, gently bring your awareness back to the present moment, carrying with you the insights and emotions that surfaced during this profound encounter.

With honesty and compassion, record your experience. Allow the pen to flow, for in these words, the dance of shadow and light continues, weaving the tapestry of integration and wholeness.

Insights Unveiled: *What insights emerged as you conversed with your shadow self? What messages did it convey?*

_____

_____

_____

Emotional Landscape: *Describe the emotions that surfaced during this journey. Were there moments of resistance, clarity, or release?*

_____

_____

_____

Resolutions and Integration: *How has this encounter with your shadow self influenced your journey towards wholeness? What steps of integration are unfolding within you?*

_____

_____

_____

Each word you've inscribed here is a step towards that sacred dance, where light and shadow merge, and the true self, in all its wholeness, emerges.

Role-Playing Scenarios

Role-playing is a dynamic approach that allows you to step into different versions of yourself, offering a mirror to observe, understand, and transform the ways your shadow self manifests in various life scenarios. Through this exercise, you'll explore your automatic reactions and envision responses aligned with your ideal self, paving the path for transformation and integration.

Scenarios

Below are specific scenarios where your shadow self might emerge. In the allocated spaces, write down your typical reactions and then describe how your ideal self would respond. Be honest and allow yourself to explore these scenarios without judgment.

Scenario 1: A colleague criticizes your work in a meeting.

Typical Reaction: *(Describe how you'd typically react in this situation.)*

_____

_____

_____

Ideal Self's Response: *(Describe how your ideal self would respond.)*

_____

_____

_____

Scenario 2: A loved one forgets an important date or event.

Typical Reaction: *(Describe how you'd typically react in this situation.)*

_____

_____

_____

Ideal Self's Response: *(Describe how your ideal self would respond.)*

_____

_____

_____

Scenario 3: You're confronted with an unexpected challenge or obstacle.

Typical Reaction: *(Describe how you'd typically react in this situation.)*

_____

_____

_____

Ideal Self's Response: *(Describe how your ideal self would respond.)*

_____

_____

_____

Now, take a moment to compare your typical reactions with the responses of your ideal self. Reflect on the differences and explore the steps towards aligning more with your ideal self.

1. Insights and Observations: (What did you notice about the differences between your typical reactions and your ideal self's responses?)

_____

_____

_____

2. Steps Towards Alignment: (What steps can you take to align more closely with your ideal self in these scenarios?)

_____

_____

_____

3. Embracing the Journey: (Reflect on the emotions and insights that arise as you envision this path of transformation.)

_____

_____

_____

Embrace this journey with compassion, for in each scenario, each reflection, you're weaving the story of your becoming, where the shadow self is not a stranger but a guide towards the luminous landscape of the self.

Breathwork Practices

Breathwork, the conscious, intentional practice of manipulating the breathing pattern, serves as a bridge connecting the conscious and subconscious realms of our being. It is a powerful tool for emotional regulation, self-awareness, and an invaluable ally in the journey of shadow work. By focusing on the breath, we can navigate the depths of our inner world, bringing light to the dark corners of our psyche and fostering a harmonious integration of all facets of the self.

Exercises

Deep Breathing Practice

1. Find a comfortable, quiet space where you can sit or lie down without interruption.
2. Place one hand on your chest and the other on your abdomen.
3. Inhale deeply through your nose, allowing your abdomen to expand, filling your lungs completely.
4. Exhale slowly through your mouth, letting all the air out and feeling your abdomen contract.
5. Repeat for 5-10 minutes.

Your Observations: *(Note your physical and emotional responses during the practice.)*

_____
_____
_____
_____
_____

Alternate Nostril Breathing

1. Sit comfortably with your spine straight and shoulders relaxed.
2. Using your right thumb, close off your right nostril.
3. Inhale deeply through your left nostril.
4. Close your left nostril with your right ring finger, releasing the right nostril.
5. Exhale through your right nostril, then inhale through the right nostril.
6. Close the right nostril and exhale through the left nostril.
7. This completes one cycle. Repeat for 5-10 cycles.

Your Observations: *(Note your physical and emotional responses during the practice.)*

_____
_____
_____
_____

Reflection Space

Impact on Emotional State: *(Reflect on how the breathwork practices influenced your emotional state. Were there any noticeable shifts or changes?)*

_____
_____
_____
_____

Insights Gained: *(What insights or realizations emerged during your practice? Did you become aware of specific emotions, thoughts, or patterns?)*

_____

_____

_____

_____

Applications in Daily Life: *(How can you integrate breathwork into your daily routine? What potential benefits do you anticipate in the context of shadow work and emotional well-being?)*

_____

_____

_____

_____

In the silent symphony of breath, each inhalation and exhalation unveils layers of the self, both shadow and light. As you immerse in these breathwork practices, embrace the revelations with openness, acknowledging that every breath is a step towards integration, healing, and wholeness. Each reflection penned down is a testament to your journey, a dance of breath and being, shadow and light, unfolding the boundless landscape of the self.

Affirmation Crafting and Reflection

Affirmations are powerful tools that aid in the transformation of the subconscious mind. These positive, present-tense statements are seeds planted in the fertile soil of our psyche, blossoming over time to overwrite negative beliefs and patterns. In the context of shadow work, affirmations become the light that illuminates the dark, the voice that speaks kindness where there was once criticism.

Follow the steps below to create affirmations that resonate with your innermost desires and challenges.

1. **Identify Negative Beliefs:** *Write down the negative beliefs or patterns you've identified in your shadow work.*

_____

_____

_____

_____

2. **Transform into Positive Statements:** *Turn each negative belief into a positive, present-tense affirmation.*

_____

_____

_____

_____

3. **Add Emotion and Imagery:** *Infuse your affirmations with emotions and vivid imagery to enhance their impact.*

_____
_____
_____
_____

4. **Reflection on Meanings:** *Reflect on the meanings of your crafted affirmations. How do they resonate with your inner self?*

_____
_____
_____
_____

Reflection Space

Week 1:

- **Affirmation Practice:** *Record the affirmations you are focusing on this week.*

_____
_____
_____

- **Impact Reflection:** *Note any shifts in mindset, emotions, or behaviors you observe.*

_____
_____
_____

Week 2:

- **Affirmation Practice:** *Record the affirmations you are focusing on this week.*

_____
_____
_____

- **Impact Reflection:** *Note any shifts in mindset, emotions, or behaviors you observe.*

_____
_____
_____

Week 3:

- **Affirmation Practice:** *Record the affirmations you are focusing on this week.*

_____
_____
_____

- **Impact Reflection:** *Note any shifts in mindset, emotions, or behaviors you observe.*

_____

_____

_____

Week 4:

- **Affirmation Practice:** *Record the affirmations you are focusing on this week.*

_____

_____

_____

- **Impact Reflection:** *Note any shifts in mindset, emotions, or behaviors you observe.*

_____

_____

_____

As you immerse yourself in this practice, allow the affirmations to become the gentle whispers that guide your steps from the shadow into the light. Each word is a beacon, illuminating the path of self-discovery, integration, and transformation. Embrace this journey with openness, for in the dance of shadow and light, every step, every word, is a celebration of the intricate, beautiful tapestry of the self.

Body Scanning Activity

Embarking on a journey within, body scanning is a bridge that connects you to the silent stories your body narrates. It's a practice that unveils the emotions, memories, and energies stored in the various corners of your physical being. In the context of shadow work, body scanning becomes a lantern, illuminating the dark recesses where the shadow self lurks, silently influencing your thoughts, emotions, and actions.

Guided Body Scanning Exercise

Close your eyes and find comfort in the silence. Breathe deeply, allowing the breath to be the gentle waves that wash the shores of your consciousness, clearing the space for introspection.

1. **Focus on Your Feet:** *Feel the sensations in your feet. Are there any emotions or resistances? Note them down.*

   _____

   _____

   _____

2. **Move to Your Legs:** *Feel the sensations in your feet. Are there any emotions or resistances? Note them down.*

   _____

   _____

   _____

3. **Your Abdomen and Chest:** *What stories do these core parts of your body tell? Write down your observations.*

_____

_____

_____

_____

4. **Arms and Hands:** *Feel into your arms and hands. Are there tensions, emotions? Record them.*

_____

_____

_____

_____

5. **Up to Your Neck and** *Head: Observe the sensations. Note the energies, emotions, or thoughts that arise.*

_____

_____

_____

_____

Reflection Space

Insights Gained: *Reflect on the emotions and sensations discovered during the body scanning. What insights have emerged about your stored emotions and their connections to your shadow self?*

_____

_____

_____

Connections to Shadow Self: *Identify any specific links between the sensations or emotions discovered and aspects of your shadow self. Are there patterns, specific emotions, or memories that are prominently coming up?*

_____

_____

_____

Steps for Releasing Stored Emotions: *Based on your insights, outline steps you can take to release stored emotions. Consider practices that resonate with you, such as breathwork, journaling, or seeking professional support.*

_____

_____

_____

Embrace this practice as a sacred dialogue between the seen and unseen aspects of yourself, a dance of light and shadow, weaving the tapestry of your complete, integrated self.

Emotional Freedom Technique

Emotional Freedom Technique (EFT Tapping) is a powerful self-help method, based on research showing that emotional trauma contributes significantly to disease. It involves tapping on specific body points while focusing on negative emotions or sensations, allowing individuals to release and transform their emotional responses to them. EFT Tapping has roots in both modern psychology and ancient Chinese acupressure techniques, combining elements of exposure therapy and cognitive reprocessing with the physical act of tapping.

In this section of your Shadow Work Journal and Workbook, you will explore EFT Tapping to navigate, manage, and transform the emotions, stress, and negative beliefs associated with your shadow self. Get ready to step into a journey where you'll learn to tap into your inner world, unlocking emotions and thoughts that are often hidden in the shadows.

Before we begin, let's note your current emotional state. Please describe your feelings, thoughts, physical sensations, and any associated emotions in the space below.

Your Emotional State Before EFT Tapping:

_____

_____

Now, follow these steps for the EFT Tapping process:

1. Identify the Issue - Write down the emotion, memory, or belief you'd like to work on:

_____

_____

_____

2. *Rate the Intensity* - On a scale of 1 to 10, how intense is the emotion or belief? [_____]

3. *Setup Affirmation:* Create an affirmation acknowledging the problem and accepting yourself. Write it here:

_____

4. *Tapping Points* - Tap each point about 5-7 times while repeating your affirmation. The points include:

- Top of the head
- Eyebrow
- Side of the eye
- Under the eye
- Under the nose
- Chin point
- Collarbone
- Under the arm

5. *Tapping Rounds:* Go through at least 3 rounds of tapping. Note any shifts or changes in your emotions and thoughts.

Your Emotional State After EFT Tapping:

_____

_____

6. *On a scale of 1 to 10, how intense is the emotion or belief now?* [____]

Reflection Space

Reflect on the differences in your emotional state before and after the EFT tapping exercise. Did the intensity of your emotions or beliefs change? Write about the shifts, insights, or realizations you experienced during this process.

_____
_____
_____
_____

Now that you've experienced EFT Tapping, consider how you might integrate this practice into your daily life. Identify specific situations, emotions, or beliefs that you can address using this technique.

_____
_____
_____
_____

Remember, EFT Tapping is a skill that you can use anytime, anywhere to manage and transform your emotions and beliefs. The more you practice, the more adept you'll become at navigating your inner world, especially those shadowy parts that often stay hidden. Each tapping session is a step towards emotional freedom, healing, and self-discovery. Make it a regular practice, and observe the transformation unfold within you.

Inner Child Healing Exercises

Every individual has an "inner child," a part of us that remains with us from childhood into adulthood, embodying our innocence, joys, fears, and childhood wounds. Our inner child influences our actions, decisions, and reactions to various life situations. In the context of shadow work, the inner child is connected to the unresolved emotions and traumas that we carry into our adult lives, often manifesting as our "shadow self."

Unhealed wounds from childhood can lead to patterns of self-sabotage, unhealthy relationships, and emotional imbalances. Thus, healing the inner child becomes a crucial step in unfolding your journey to self-awareness, self-love, and overall wellness. In this section, we will guide you through exercises designed to help you connect with, understand, and heal your inner child.

1. **Visualize Your Inner Child:**

Close your eyes and visualize your inner child. See their face, expressions, and surroundings. Take note of what they are feeling and experiencing.

_____

_____

_____

_____

_____

_____

_____

2. Dialogue with Your Inner Child:

Write a letter to your inner child. Ask them about their fears, joys, and unmet needs. Let them express freely.

_____

_____

_____

_____

_____

_____

_____

3. Respond to Your Inner Child:

Now, respond to your inner child from your current adult perspective. Assure them, provide comfort, and address their feelings and needs.

_____

_____

_____

_____

_____

_____

_____

4. Healing Actions:

Identify specific actions you can take to meet the needs and heal the wounds of your inner child.

_____

_____

_____

_____

Reflection Space

Reflect on the emotions and insights that emerged during the inner child healing exercises. Did you discover unmet needs or unresolved emotions? How do you feel about your inner child now? Write about the realizations, feelings, and resolutions that have arisen.

_____

_____

_____

_____

Take this journey of healing your inner child with patience and love. Recognize that this is a process of unfolding, understanding, and healing. The path to wholeness involves embracing every part of yourself, especially the tender, vulnerable inner child within. Revisit these exercises as often as needed, each time peeling back another layer, getting closer to the core of your true self, unburdened and free.

Visualization Techniques

Visualization is a potent tool for shadow work. It allows us to create a mental image of our shadow self, the part of us harboring unresolved emotions, suppressed desires, and unexplored aspects. By visualizing, we can safely observe, interact, and integrate these aspects, transforming negative beliefs and emotions into profound insights and positive changes. This technique creates a bridge between the conscious and unconscious mind, fostering healing, wholeness, and inner harmony.

1. **Meeting Your Shadow** - *Relax and close your eyes. Imagine yourself walking down a path leading to a serene and safe space where your shadow self-resides. As you meet your shadow, observe its form, features, and expressions.*

_____

_____

_____

_____

2. **Conversation with the Shadow** - *Engage in a dialogue with your shadow self. Ask questions, listen, and allow it to express its feelings, desires, fears, and needs without judgment.*

_____

_____

_____

_____

3. **Integrating the Shadow** - *Visualize embracing your shadow, acknowledging its presence as a part of you. Feel the integration, the acceptance, and the completeness that comes with it.*

_____
_____
_____
_____
_____

Reflection Space

Reflect on the visualization experience. What emotions and insights emerged as you met, conversed, and integrated your shadow self? How can these insights inform your journey to self-discovery and healing? Write down emotions experienced, insights gained and steps for ongoing practice.

_____
_____
_____
_____
_____

Visualization is an ongoing journey. The insights and transformations you'll experience will evolve and deepen over time. Revisit these exercises to continue exploring, understanding, and integrating your shadow self, fostering a path to self-discovery, healing, and wholeness. Each visualization is a step closer to inner harmony, self-acceptance, and the unification of all parts of your being.

Somatic Experiencing Tasks

Somatic experiencing is a body-oriented approach to the healing of trauma and other stress disorders. This technique emphasizes the exploration and release of physical tension that remains in the aftermath of trauma. By focusing on bodily sensations, we can unearth, process, and release stored emotions associated with the shadow self, paving the way for healing and integration.

Tuning into Bodily Sensations - *Sit in a quiet space, close your eyes, and focus on your breathing. Gradually shift your attention to different parts of your body. Notice any sensations, emotions, or resistances and Record Your Observations:*

_____

_____

_____

_____

Identifying Emotions Linked to Sensations: *For each sensation noticed, explore any associated emotions. Allow yourself to feel without judgement and Record the Emotions and Sensations:*

_____

_____

_____

_____

Observing Resistances: *Identify any resistances or blocks in acknowledging or feeling the sensations and emotions. Be curious, explore their origin, and Record Your Observations:*

_____

_____

_____

_____

Insights Gained: *Explore the insights gained from noticing and acknowledging your bodily sensations and linked emotions. How do these insights contribute to understanding your shadow self? Record Your Insights:*

_____

_____

_____

_____

Steps for Healing and Integration: *Based on your insights, outline steps to address, release, and integrate the noticed sensations and emotions, fostering healing and wholeness. Record Your Steps for Healing:*

_____

_____

_____

_____

Cognitive Restructuring Exercises

Cognitive restructuring is a therapeutic process that aids in identifying, challenging, and altering negative beliefs, thoughts, and patterns. Often, the shadow self is associated with deeply entrenched negative beliefs that can impact our emotions and behaviors. In this exercise, you will learn to pinpoint, assess, and transform these beliefs into empowering thoughts, fostering healing and integration.

Identifying Negative Beliefs - *Reflect on a situation where you experienced intense emotions. Identify the underlying beliefs that fueled these emotions. Avoid judgment, and Record Your Beliefs:*

_____

_____

_____

_____

Challenging the Beliefs - *Question the validity and basis of these beliefs. Are they absolute truths, or can they be challenged? Explore evidence that contradicts them and Record Your Findings:*

_____

_____

_____

_____

Reframing the Beliefs - *Create new, empowering beliefs to replace the identified negative ones. Consider how these new beliefs can transform your emotional responses and behaviors and Record Your New Beliefs*

_____

_____

_____

_____

Emotional and Behavioral Changes - *Explore any changes in your emotions and behaviors resulting from the cognitive restructuring. What differences do you observe? Record the Changes:*

_____

_____

_____

_____

Path Forward - *Based on your reflections, outline further steps to nurture and strengthen these new, empowering beliefs. How will you integrate them into your daily life? Record Your Steps Forward:*

_____

_____

_____

_____

Progressive Muscle Relaxation Guide

Progressive Muscle Relaxation (PMR) is a method where individuals learn to notice and release tension in various muscle groups throughout the body. This practice is not just physical; as the body relaxes, the mind follows, aiding in the release of stored emotions and mental stress. In the realm of shadow work, PMR can be an essential tool to access, understand, and release physical manifestations of emotional pain and trauma.

Preparing for Relaxation - *Find a quiet and comfortable place to sit or lie down. Close your eyes, take a few deep breaths, and center your focus inward. Be aware of your overall physical and emotional state before starting and Record Your Initial State:*

_____

Progressive Muscle Relaxation Steps: Progressively tense, then relax, each muscle group in your body, starting from your toes up to your head. Pay close attention to the sensations during tension and relaxation.

Toes and Feet - *Tense and relax, then Record Sensations and Emotional Releases:*

_____

_____

Legs and Thighs - *Tense and relax, then Record Sensations and Emotional Releases*

_____

_____

Abdomen and Chest - *Tense and relax, then Record Sensations and Emotional Releases:*

_____

_____

Arms and Hands - *Tense and relax, then Record Sensations and Emotional Releases:*

_____

_____

Face and Head - *Tense and relax, then Record Sensations and Emotional Releases:*

_____

_____

Reflection Space: *Reflect on the changes in your physical sensations and emotional state, the insights gained about your shadow self from stored tensions, and how PMR can be integrated into your daily routine for ongoing stress and emotion management. Record Your Comprehensive Reflections:*

_____

_____

_____

_____

Sound Healing Guide

Sound healing is a transformative practice that utilizes the power of sound frequencies to restore balance and harmony within the body, mind, and spirit. It can be especially potent in the realm of shadow work, offering a unique pathway to access, explore, and integrate repressed or unacknowledged aspects of the self. The vibrations of sound can penetrate deep into the psyche, unveiling and healing the hidden corners of our existence.

Binaural Beats - *Listen to a binaural beats track designed for shadow work or emotional healing. With headphones on, allow the distinct frequencies in each ear to synchronize your brainwaves. Pay close attention to your emotional and psychological responses and Record Your Experience:*

_____

_____

_____

_____

Chanting or Mantra Meditation - *Engage in a chanting or mantra meditation. Choose a specific mantra that resonates with your shadow work journey. As you chant, notice the vibrations and their effects on your body and mind. Record Your Experience*

_____

_____

_____

_____

Singing Bowls - *Listen to or play singing bowls, focusing on the harmonic tones and vibrations. Observe the sensations within your body, the emotions that arise, and the thoughts that come to the surface. Record Your Experience:*

_____

_____

_____

_____

Reflection Space:

Reflect on the effects of sound healing on your mental and emotional states, the insights gained about your shadow self, and how you can incorporate sound healing into your daily practice for ongoing relaxation and healing. Record Your Comprehensive Reflections:

_____

_____

_____

_____

Sound healing is a harmonious journey that intertwines with the intricate dance of shadow work. The vibrational energies not only touch the physical being but reverberate into the depths of the psyche, unveiling, and healing the concealed aspects of self. Revisit these practices, allowing each session to deepen your awareness and catalyze your journey towards holistic integration and well-being.

Shadow Integration Rituals

Rituals have been a cornerstone in psychological and spiritual practices for centuries, acting as bridges to deeper realms of consciousness. In the context of shadow work, rituals facilitate the acknowledgment, acceptance, and transformation of the shadow self. They create a sacred space where suppressed emotions and aspects can emerge, be honored, and integrated, fostering holistic well-being.

Candle Ritual - *Light a candle to symbolize the illumination of your shadow self. As you focus on the flame, allow suppressed emotions and thoughts to surface. Acknowledge them without judgment and Record Your Experience:*

_____

_____

_____

Writing and Burning Ritual - *Write down the aspects of your shadow self that you're ready to acknowledge and transform. Read them aloud, then safely burn the paper as a symbolic release. As the smoke rises, visualize these aspects being transformed by light. Record Your Experience*

_____

_____

_____

Guided Shadow Visualization: *Engage in a guided meditation focusing on meeting your shadow self. Visualize a safe space where you can communicate openly and with compassion. Ask your shadow what it needs for integration and healing. Listen attentively and Record Your Experience:*

_____

_____

_____

Reflection Space:

Reflect on the transformation and insights gained through these rituals. How have these practices influenced your perception and relationship with your shadow self? What steps will you take to continue this journey of acknowledgment, acceptance, and integration? Record Your Comprehensive Reflections:

_____

_____

_____

_____

Each ritual in shadow work serves as a gateway to deeper self-understanding and healing. As you regularly engage in these practices, anticipate a transformative journey where every acknowledgment, every acceptance, and every integration brings you closer to the core of authentic and holistic existence. Your shadow, once veiled in darkness, can become a source of light, strength, and wholeness.

Gratitude Practices

In the intricate journey of shadow work, gratitude serves as a balancing force, illuminating the spaces of light amidst the darkness. Embracing gratitude can transform the narrative of the shadow self, offering a perspective where every aspect, including the repressed and denied, is a part of the holistic self. This section guides you through incorporating gratitude practices, paving the path for balanced integration.

Gratitude Journaling - *Each day, dedicate a moment to jot down three things you are grateful for. It can be as simple as the warmth of the sun or as profound as a loved one's embrace. Record Your Daily Gratitudes:*

- Day 1:

- Day 2:

- Day 3:

- Day 4:

- Day 5:

(Continue this pattern for as long as you need.)

Gratitude Meditation - *Engage in a daily meditation focusing on something you're thankful for. Visualize this element, embrace the emotions associated with it, and observe the shifts in your emotional state. Record Your Emotional Shifts:*

- Session 1:
  _____

- Session 2:
  _____

- Session 3:
  _____

(Continue this pattern for each session.)

Reflection Space:

Reflect on the influence of these gratitude practices on your emotional state, perspective, and the journey of integrating the shadow self. Have negative emotions or perspectives shifted? What insights have emerged in the process of acknowledging the positive amidst the shadow? Record Your Comprehensive Reflections:

_____

_____

_____

_____

Gratitude, with its gentle yet profound power, has the capacity to transform the shadow's dense spaces into areas of light and learning. As you delve deeper into this practice, let each acknowledgment of gratitude be a beam of light, casting shadows yet also illuminating them, allowing for a balanced, compassionate, and holistic journey of self-discovery and integration.

The Power of Shared Journeys

"Every shadow no matter how deep is threatened by morning light." - Trent Jamieson

The path of shadow work is profound, transformative, and deeply personal. Yet, despite the solitary nature of this introspective journey, there's a collective resonance in the experiences we all share. Before diving into the depths of shadow work, many of us felt lost in the vast labyrinth of our emotions and memories, searching for clarity and understanding in a world that often seemed overwhelming.

You, dear reader, chose this book as a beacon on your journey, and I hope it has been a guiding light, helping you navigate the intricate tapestry of your inner world. But remember, just as you sought guidance, there are countless others standing at the crossroads, yearning for the same insights and tools that you now possess.

Imagine the power of knowing that your insights, your revelations, and even your challenges could light the way for someone else on a similar journey. Your experience, your voice, can be the very beacon another soul needs.

By taking a few moments to share your honest feedback and reflections on this workbook, you are not only helping Megan and future readers refine and appreciate the guidance provided but also letting countless others know they are not alone on this path. Through your words, they'll find hope, camaraderie, and the assurance that there's a community ready to support them.

Leaving a review is a simple yet powerful gesture. It's an opportunity to amplify the message of transformation and healing, ensuring that more and more people can harness the transformative power of shadow work.

In this vast universe of stories and experiences, your voice matters. Let it be heard, let it resonate, and let it be a beacon for all those who seek the light amidst their shadows.

With immense gratitude for your journey and your voice, Megan Walls.

Part 3:
Shadow Work Prompts

The path of self-exploration is paved with questions. Questions that gently tug at the veils of our unconscious, encouraging what lies beneath to emerge and be acknowledged. In this pivotal third part, we journey through an array of curated prompts, designed to act as guiding lights that shine into the intricate caverns of our psyche, illuminating areas we may have consciously or unconsciously sidestepped.

But why are prompts so essential in shadow work? Picture them as keys. Each question has the potential to unlock a door within, leading to a room filled with memories, emotions, traumas, joys, and fears. These rooms, once opened, allow us the chance to tidy, heal, or sometimes, simply sit and understand their contents.

The prompts you will encounter here are more than mere questions; they are invitations. Invitations to introspect about our traumas, to reflect on the nuanced dynamics of our workplace relationships, to delve into the depths of our spiritual beliefs, and even to confront our fears and anxieties about the future. They encompass the vast tapestry of human experience, ensuring that no thread remains unexamined.

Whether it's addressing the roots of body image issues or exploring the foundations of our financial beliefs, each set of prompts within this part is meticulously structured to guide you through a specific facet of your life. While some might resonate deeply and elicit a flood of memories and emotions, others may offer a moment of silent contemplation. Regardless of the immediate reaction, know that each prompt is a stepping stone towards deeper self-awareness.

Prompts for Trauma

Describe a specific traumatic event and the emotions it evokes when you recall it. How has it impacted your daily life?

_____
_____
_____
_____

What coping mechanisms have you developed in response to this trauma? Evaluate their effectiveness in your healing process.

_____
_____
_____
_____

Explore and write about the triggers that cause you to relive or remember the traumatic experience. How do you typically respond to these triggers?

_____
_____
_____
_____

How has the trauma affected your relationships with others and yourself? Identify any patterns of isolation, anxiety, or distrust.

_____
_____
_____
_____

Identify and write about any physical sensations or reactions you experience when recalling the trauma. How do these sensations connect to your emotional state?

_____
_____
_____
_____

Explore any steps you've taken towards healing from the trauma. What has been beneficial, and what challenges still remain?

_____
_____
_____
_____

Prompts for Career and Workplace

Reflect on a challenging experience or conflict at your workplace. What emotions and thoughts did it evoke?

How do your personal values align or conflict with your workplace culture? Describe specific situations where this has been evident.

Identify a time when you felt particularly valued or undervalued at work. How did these experiences affect your job performance and self-esteem?

Explore the role of your shadow self in your professional life. Are there behaviors or reactions you wish to change or understand better?

How do you handle workplace stress and pressure? Describe the coping mechanisms and their effectiveness.

Write about your career aspirations and any fears or uncertainties associated with them. How might these be connected to your shadow self?

Prompts for Spirituality

Describe a moment of spiritual doubt or questioning. What triggered this and how did it make you feel?

Explore how your upbringing or early life experiences influenced your current spiritual beliefs. Are there aspects you're revisiting or challenging?

Identify and reflect on a spiritual experience that had a profound impact on you. How did it affect your beliefs and emotions?

How does your shadow self interact with your spirituality? Are there suppressed aspects that emerge during spiritual practices or reflections?

Consider a spiritual teaching or principle that you find challenging to fully embrace. Explore the emotions and resistances that arise.

Write about your spiritual goals and the barriers you face in reaching them. How can you address and integrate these challenges into your spiritual journey?

Prompts for Relationships

Reflect on a relationship that triggers strong emotions in you. What are these emotions and how do you typically handle them?

Consider a recurring pattern or issue in your relationships. What underlying beliefs or past experiences might be contributing to this pattern?

Recall a significant conflict in a relationship and explore your role in it. What did the conflict reveal about your hidden fears or desires?

Describe a time when you felt vulnerable in a relationship. How did you react, and what did this reveal about your shadow self?

Explore the impact of your family dynamics on your relationships. Are there shadow aspects rooted in your early family experiences?

Identify a relationship where you feel most challenged. What aspects of your shadow self can you recognize and seek to understand through this relationship?

Prompts for Self-Esteem and Self-Worth

Recall a specific moment where you felt a significant lack of self-esteem. What triggered this feeling and how did it manifest in your behavior?

Explore the narrative you hold about your worthiness. How has this been shaped by past experiences or messages from others?

Identify the criticisms you often tell yourself. Consider their origins and the impact they have on your emotional well-being.

Reflect on a situation where you undermined your skills or achievements. What beliefs about yourself were reinforced by this?

Consider the role of comparison in your life. How does comparing yourself to others affect your self-esteem and self-perception?

Analyze a positive achievement or compliment that you found hard to accept. Explore the underlying beliefs and emotions that surfaced at that moment.

Prompts for Body Image

Reflect on how your body image affects your self-esteem and daily interactions. Can you trace these feelings back to a specific event or period in your life?

Explore any societal or cultural standards of beauty that influence your perception of your body. How have these external factors shaped your internal narrative?

Recall an experience where you felt extremely self-conscious about your body. What emotions and thoughts were prevalent at that time?

Identify the positive aspects of your body that you often overlook. What mental barriers prevent you from acknowledging and appreciating these aspects?

How does your shadow self influence your relationship with your body? Explore the hidden emotions and beliefs that surface in moments of body dissatisfaction.

Consider a moment where you felt complete acceptance of your body. What can this experience reveal about the steps needed to improve your body image and self-esteem?

Prompts for Mental Health and Well-Being

Reflect on a period of emotional distress or mental health challenge. What thoughts and emotions were most prevalent, and how did you cope?

Explore the coping mechanisms you've adopted during times of mental health struggles. Evaluate their effectiveness and potential areas for improvement.

Identify any stigmas or societal beliefs that impact your perception and treatment of your mental health. How can you challenge and transform these beliefs?

Consider the role of your shadow self in your mental health journey. How might unacknowledged aspects of yourself influence your mental well-being?

Describe a moment of breakthrough or significant insight in your mental health journey. What did it reveal about your strengths and areas for growth?

Explore the relationship between your mental health and physical well-being. How do the mind and body interact, and how can you nurture this connection?

Prompts for Childhood Memories and Upbringing

Recall a childhood memory that continues to influence your emotions and behaviors today. What emotions are attached to this memory?

Explore the parental messages or family dynamics that shaped your self-perception and worldview. How do these elements manifest in your current life?

Identify a positive childhood experience. How did this moment shape your values, and how can it be a source of strength in addressing your shadow self?

Reflect on a recurring theme or pattern in your childhood memories. What insight does this pattern offer into the formation of your shadow aspects?

Consider a moment of childhood rebellion or defiance. What were you resisting, and what does this reveal about your unmet needs or suppressed emotions?

Explore the influence of your upbringing on your adult relationships and self-esteem. How can acknowledging this connection facilitate shadow work and healing?

Prompts for Grief and Loss

Reflect on a significant loss you've experienced. How has this loss impacted your emotions, beliefs, and behaviors?

Explore the emotions that surface when you think about this loss. Are there feelings you haven't fully acknowledged or processed?

Describe any changes in your identity or self-perception resulting from this loss. How has your shadow self responded to these changes?

Consider coping strategies you've adopted to deal with grief. Identify which ones are helpful and which ones might be hindering your healing process.

Reflect on a moment of intense emotion related to your loss. What insights can this moment provide about your deeper fears, needs, or desires?

Explore the connection between your grief and your physical well-being. How does your body respond to the emotions associated with loss, and what does this reveal about your shadow self?

Prompts for Personal Development and Growth

Reflect on a significant achievement in your personal development. What internal obstacles did you overcome, and what aspects of your shadow self were revealed?

Explore a personal goal that seems daunting. What underlying beliefs or fears are associated with this goal?

Identify a moment of failure or setback. What emotions and beliefs surfaced, and how can these insights facilitate growth?

Consider a skill or quality you wish to develop. What internal barriers exist, and how might these be linked to your shadow self?

Reflect on the role of criticism in your growth. How do you respond to criticism, and what does this reveal about your hidden insecurities or fears?

Explore a transformative experience that led to personal growth. What aspects of your shadow self were integrated or confronted during this transformation?

Prompts for Social and Cultural Conditioning

Reflect on a societal or cultural norm that you find yourself adhering to. How does it align or conflict with your personal beliefs and values?

_____
_____
_____
_____

Explore a moment when you became aware of the impact of social conditioning on your thoughts or behaviors. What emotions or realizations surfaced?

_____
_____
_____
_____

Identify a belief or attitude instilled by your cultural background. How has this influenced your shadow self and your personal development?

_____
_____
_____
_____

Consider the role of media and societal narratives in shaping your self-perception. What aspects of yourself have been suppressed or influenced by these external factors?

Reflect on a time you challenged a societal or cultural expectation. What did this reveal about your hidden desires, beliefs, or values?

Explore how social and cultural conditioning has influenced your relationships and interactions with others. How can recognizing this influence facilitate your shadow work?

Prompts for Fear and Anxiety

What's a recurring fear that seems to control some of your behaviors or decisions? Dive deep into its origins and impact on your life.

Imagine facing this fear head-on; what emotions and thoughts surface? How might confronting it lead to personal growth?

Discuss an experience where anxiety took over. What were the underlying beliefs or thoughts fueling this anxiety?

How does your physical body react during moments of fear or anxiety? Explore the connection between these physical sensations and your emotional state.

Identify a situation where fear or anxiety held you back. What would have been different if these emotions weren't in the picture?

Explore any patterns or themes in your fears and anxieties. How might these be connected to unacknowledged aspects of yourself?

Prompts for Anger and Forgiveness

Describe a moment of intense anger. What triggered it, and what did you uncover about your underlying emotions or unresolved issues?

How do you generally cope with anger? Reflect on the effectiveness and healthiness of these coping strategies.

Consider a person you need to forgive, or who needs to forgive you. What emotions and obstacles arise when you think of forgiveness in this context?

Explore the underlying emotions that often accompany your anger. Are there patterns revealing unresolved issues or suppressed feelings?

Identify a situation where you felt wronged or mistreated. How has holding onto this experience impacted your emotional wellbeing and relationships?

What changes do you anticipate in your emotional landscape and relationships by fully expressing and managing anger, and embracing forgiveness?

Prompts for Future Aspirations and Anxieties

Envision your ideal future. What emotions arise, and are there any fears or anxieties associated with achieving this vision?

Consider a specific goal for your future. What internal or external obstacles do you anticipate, and how might your shadow self be involved?

How do your anxieties about the future influence your present actions and decisions? Dive deep into specific instances.

Identify a past experience where anxiety about the future affected your performance or wellbeing. What lessons did you learn?

Explore the root of your most significant anxiety about the future. How is it connected to your beliefs, past experiences, or shadow self?

What would a future free of this anxiety look like? Visualize and describe the changes in your emotions, behaviors, and life trajectory.

Prompts for Financial Beliefs and Behaviors

Dive into a memory where money caused stress or tension. What underlying beliefs about money were revealed?

How were your financial beliefs shaped during your upbringing? Identify specific incidents or messages that left a lasting impact.

Examine a financial goal that feels out of reach. What internal barriers or beliefs are hindering your progress?

Reflect on a financial decision you regret. What were the driving emotions or beliefs behind that choice?

Consider your financial habits. Are there patterns that align with or contradict your values and aspirations?

How does money influence your sense of self-worth and security? Explore the emotional and psychological ties between your finances and self-perception.

Prompts for Health and Wellness

Identify a health goal you're striving for. Explore the emotions and beliefs that either fuel or hinder your journey towards this goal.

Reflect on your body's signals and messages. Are there specific symptoms or sensations that you've been ignoring or suppressing?

Describe a moment when stress, anxiety, or emotional turmoil manifested physically. Explore the connection between your mental and physical state.

How do your eating, exercise, and sleep habits reflect your emotional well-being? Identify patterns and their underlying causes.

Consider a health or wellness challenge you've faced. What did it reveal about your strengths, vulnerabilities, and the role of your shadow self?

Explore the impact of social and cultural influences on your health and wellness beliefs. How have these external factors shaped your internal narrative?

Prompts for Creativity and Expression

Reflect on a moment when you felt highly creative. What internal or external factors facilitated this surge of creativity?

Identify a creative block you've experienced. Explore the underlying emotions and beliefs that contributed to this obstacle.

How does your shadow self influence your creative expression? Are there suppressed feelings or thoughts that emerge through creativity?

Describe a piece of art, music, writing, or other creative works that deeply moved you. What emotions or insights did it awaken?

Consider your unexpressed creative desires. What holds you back from exploring and expressing these aspects of yourself?

Explore the role of criticism and validation in your creative journey. How do these external factors impact your creative self-esteem and expression?

Prompts for Decision Making and Regrets

Think of a decision you made that you later regretted. Explore the emotions and beliefs that influenced that choice.

How does fear or anxiety influence your decision-making processes? Provide specific examples.

Reflect on a decision where your intuition or inner voice guided you. How did it turn out, and what did you learn about yourself?

Consider a time when you avoided making a decision. What was at stake, and what emotions or beliefs were in play?

Explore a pattern in your decision-making that you'd like to change. How is your shadow self involved in this pattern?

Reflect on a decision that led to unexpected outcomes, positive or negative. What insights did you gain about your decision-making processes and underlying beliefs?

Prompts for Boundaries and Personal Space

Recall a situation where your boundaries were challenged or violated. How did you respond, and what did it reveal about your self-worth and assertiveness?

How do your boundaries change in different relationships and settings? Explore the flexibility and firmness of your boundaries.

Identify a boundary you find difficult to maintain. What underlying emotions or beliefs make this boundary challenging?

Consider a time when you respected someone else's boundaries. How did it influence the relationship and your understanding of your own boundaries?

Reflect on the origins of your boundaries. Are they rooted in past experiences, fears, or values, and how might they be connected to your shadow self?

Explore a situation where establishing a boundary led to personal growth or improved relationships. What did you learn about your needs and values?

Prompts for Dreams and Subconscious Thoughts

Recall a recent dream that evoked strong emotions or confusion. Explore its symbols, themes, and possible connections to your current life challenges or desires.

How do your dreams reflect your suppressed or unexpressed emotions and desires? Provide examples and delve into their meanings.

Consider a recurring dream theme or symbol. How might this repetition be connected to unresolved issues or your shadow self?

Reflect on a dream that led to an insight or revelation about a personal challenge or aspiration. Explore the transformation that followed this realization.

Identify the emotions you often wake up with after dreaming. What might these emotions reveal about your subconscious processing and shadow aspects?

Explore a nightmare or unsettling dream. What fears, anxieties, or suppressed emotions might be surfacing through this dream?

Part 4:
Triggers Identification

As you venture deeper into the realms of shadow work, you'll encounter a landscape rich in transformative experiences, insights, and the occasional challenges. Among these, understanding and navigating your 'triggers' will emerge as a pivotal phase of your journey.

What lies ahead is not just a simple exercise. It is a gateway. A portal that will usher you into a deeper communion with yourself. As you turn each page and answer every prompt, anticipate layers of past emotions, buried memories, and dormant reactions to unveil themselves. This is not a mere recounting of events but an exploration into the intricate tapestry of your psyche.

The Trigger Resolution page you're about to engage with is designed not just to uncover, but to empower. The prompts are your guiding stars, leading you to not only identify and understand your triggers but to reimagine your relationship with them. As you delve deeper, envision a future where you're no longer at the mercy of unexplored emotions, but one where you stand resilient, understanding, and in control.

And as you contemplate the advice you'd offer a loved one, you'll find yourself at a crossroads of empathy and self-realization. It's here that you'll recognize the innate wisdom you possess and the compassion you're capable of extending, not just to others, but crucially, to yourself.

By the end of this exercise, anticipate a shift. A transformation from uncertainty to clarity, from reactivity to understanding, and from past entanglements to future possibilities.

So, as you prepare to pen down your thoughts and feelings, know that with every word, you're scripting a future filled with emotional freedom, self-assurance, and profound self-understanding. Here's to your transformative journey.

To help with this, find an example of a "Trigger Resolution" page, filled out by an individual as they navigate a specific trigger in their life:

Trigger Resolution – Sample Page

What event or circumstance triggered you? Briefly describe the situation.

A coworker made a passing comment about my presentation style, saying it was "too relaxed."

What were the first emotions you felt?

Hurt, embarrassment, self-doubt.

Reflect on any past experiences or memories this trigger might be linked to.

I remember my teacher in 5th grade criticizing my speech in front of the whole class, telling me I lacked seriousness.

What might be the deeper meaning or fear behind this trigger for you?

I fear not being seen as competent or professional. I'm worried that people won't take me seriously.

If someone you cared about had this trigger, what would you say to them?"

"Everyone has their own style, and it's what makes them unique. It's possible to be relaxed and still be professional. Besides, it's just one person's opinion."

How can you turn the insight gained from this trigger into a positive action or change?

I will seek feedback from multiple sources about my presentation style to get a balanced view. I'll also attend a workshop to refine my skills, ensuring I am confident in my unique style.

Trigger Resolution

What event or circumstance triggered you? Briefly describe the situation.

What were the first emotions you felt?

Reflect on any past experiences or memories this trigger might be linked to.

What might be the deeper meaning or fear behind this trigger for you?

If someone you cared about had this trigger, what would you say to them?"

How can you turn the insight gained from this trigger into a positive action or change?

Part 5:
Integrating the Shadow

Embarking on the final and perhaps most transformative leg of our journey, Part 5 focuses on the art and science of shadow integration. Here, we shift our perspective from mere recognition and understanding to active assimilation, bringing together the disparate parts of ourselves into a cohesive, harmonious whole.

Shadow work is not solely about diving into the dark recesses of our minds; it's also about illuminating these areas, reconciling with them, and incorporating them into our conscious understanding. To "integrate" is to combine one thing with another so they become a whole. In the context of shadow work, it means taking all that we've learned about our hidden self and weaving it seamlessly into the tapestry of who we are.

In this essential part of the book, we delve into specific strategies and techniques aimed at fostering a profound sense of self-acceptance. We'll explore exercises rooted in compassion, forgiveness, and conscious tension release, laying the groundwork for personal growth and genuine self-awareness. We traverse the spectrum of human emotion, from confronting and processing pain to reveling in the joy of personal transformation and growth.

You'll also discover the benefits and challenges of maintaining emotional and psychological balance, a crucial aspect of shadow integration. And ultimately, we will guide you towards finding non-situational happiness—a state of inner joy and contentment that's not tethered to external events or circumstances.

Acceptance and Compassion

In the quiet recesses of our mind, there exists a self, often unacknowledged, buried beneath the layers of our conscious personality - the shadow self. This elusive part of our being is as integral as the person we consciously present to the world. Accepting the existence of our shadow self is the first, yet pivotal step in a journey towards a harmonious and balanced life.

Sarah, for instance, lived a life brimming with accolades and admiration. A woman with achievements that sparkled, and a personality that radiated confidence. Yet, there was an undercurrent of restlessness, an inexplicable void, rooted in the denial of parts of herself that she deemed unacceptable. Sarah was exemplary in her professional life but haunted by an inexplicable anxiety and dissatisfaction in her personal life. She was trapped in the cycle of denial – an evasion of her shadow self.

The realization of her imbalances unfolded during a silent retreat, where Sarah was confronted with the neglected aspects of her psyche. It was a confrontation with the unvoiced fears, repressed desires, and unresolved conflicts that lay dormant, yet powerful in the unfrequented corridors of her soul. The first crack of dawn in her shadow work journey was not an accumulation of more accolades, but an acceptance of the imperfections and the dark recesses of her self.

This narrative mirrors many of our lives. We meticulously shape and polish our exterior selves, becoming prisoners of the images we project, and hostages to the expectations that accompany them. However, liberation commences with acceptance. In the embracing of the darkness, we unshackle ourselves from the imprisonment of pretense and step into the light of authenticity.

So, how does one journey from denial to acceptance?

An exploration into the realms of the subconscious mind is akin to delving into a forest shrouded in darkness. It is not the absence of light that is daunting but the fear of what the light may reveal. The initial steps are often immersed in resistance. However, denial is akin to nurturing a silent storm. Suppression breeds turmoil, an emotional whirlwind that manifests in unexpected and often undesired ways.

One practical approach to foster acceptance involves conscious reflection. Engaging in activities like journaling, that allow the unfurling of the subconscious into the conscious realm, aids in illuminating the aspects of the self, darkened by neglect and denial. When the ink meets paper, unvoiced emotions and unacknowledged thoughts converge, offering insights into the hidden recesses of the soul.

As with Sarah's realization, an aspect of shadow work is the confrontation with elements of the self that are in disarray. In this confrontation, there is an unraveling of complex emotional architectures. A confrontation not borne from conflict, but from a space of curiosity and openness to explore, unravel, and understand.

Embracing the shadow is a recognition of its existence. It's a dance with vulnerability and an intimate engagement with the fragments of the self, often disconnected, yet yearning for acknowledgment. In acceptance, there is not a dissolution of the shadow but an integration, a weaving of the dark and light fibers of the being into a tapestry of wholesomeness and balance.

Through acceptance, the veils of denial are lifted, and the journey of shadow work commences. In the acknowledgment of the shadow, there's an unearthing of buried potentials, an illumination of dark corners, and an integration that fosters a symphony of balance – a dance between the conscious and subconscious, light and dark, visible and invisible aspects of the self. Herein, lays the foundation of shadow work – an odyssey from fragmented existence to holistic living.

Cultivating Compassion in Shadow Work

In the enlightening journey of exploring the shadow self, a companion as steadfast and illuminating as the torchbearer in darkened corridors, is compassion. While acceptance is the opening of doors to the shadowed realms of our psyche, compassion is the gentle hand that guides us through the intricate and often tumultuous pathways of this intimate exploration.

Let's consider Alex, a high-performing executive who appeared to have conquered professional summits. Yet beneath this exterior, lay a tormented soul, tangled in the thorns of unexpressed emotions and traumatic memories. The journey of acceptance was marked, but the road to integration was blocked by internalized criticism and an incapacitating self-judgment.

Enter compassion.

The grace of compassion transformed Alex's shadow work from a confrontational battle into a nurturing and enlightening journey. Compassion isn't an erasure of the shadow; instead, it's a nurturing embrace, a soft whisper that articulates acceptance and seeks to understand, heal, and integrate.

The cultivation of self-compassion is akin to tenderly tending a garden. Each emotion, thought, and aspect of the self, even those ensnared in the shadow, are flowers waiting to bloom. But how does one nurture this garden of the self with the waters of compassion?

Strategy 1: Mindfulness Meditation

In the realm of emotional chaos, silence is a sanctuary. Mindfulness meditation is not just a pause but a profound plunge into the silent, yet articulate realms of the self. It is in this silence that the whispers of the shadow find a voice, and in this echoing, compassion finds expression.

Strategy 2: The Companion of Journaling

Where words falter in vocal expression, they dance gracefully upon the pages of a journal. Journaling in the shadow work is not just an articulation but a dialogue - a conversation where compassion listens, speaks, and nurtures. It is a space where judgment is replaced by understanding, and suppression by expression.

Strategy 3: The Therapy of Nature

Nature, in its silent eloquence, speaks the language of compassion. A walk in the embrace of nature is not an escape but a return. A return to the innate harmony where the tumult of the shadow finds solace, and compassion emerges from the silent conversations between the soul and the rustling leaves.

Strategy 4: The Art of Self-Care

Compassion is also a tangible act. The rituals of self-care – be it a nurturing meal, a healing massage, or a soulful melody, are articulations of compassion. It's a non-verbal dialogue where the self communicates value, worth, and love to the shadowed aspects yearning for acknowledgment.

As Alex unfolded the pages of his journal, meditated in the silent embrace of dawn, walked through the nurturing trails of nature, and indulged in acts of self-care, a transformation ensued. The shadowed emotions and memories, once tormented, now found a nurturing embrace. Each emotion was not a prisoner but a guest, welcomed, listened to, and embraced with compassion.

In the crucible of compassion, the tumultuous waves of the shadow find calm. It's a sanctuary where acceptance evolves into integration. The darkness isn't eradicated but illuminated. Every fear, inadequacy, and suppressed desire isn't vanquished but understood, and in this understanding, a harmonious dance between the shadow and the light emerges.

In the compassionate embrace, the shadow isn't an adversary but a companion, contributing its silent, yet potent voice to the symphony of our holistic self. Here, in the nurturing bosom of compassion, the journey of shadow work finds not just a path but a graceful dance of integration, healing, and wholesomeness.

The Transformation through Acceptance and Compassion

Acceptance and compassion, though distinct, are symbiotic in the artistry of shadow work. They converge, crafting a pathway that isn't just about the unearthing of the repressed self, but the genesis of a profound transformation characterized by self-awareness, emotional healing, and a transcendental personal growth.

The embrace of the shadow self is not an end, but a beginning – a precipice from where the soul takes its flight into spaces of elevated consciousness and enriched existence. Maria's journey, akin to many who have valiantly ventured into the spaces of their inner worlds, is a testament to this transformative odyssey.

Maria, a woman of assertive presence, always knew of the existence of a silent undercurrent, a whispering shadow that echoed the sentiments of inadequacy and fears, suppressed yet incessantly vocal in the silent nights of soulful contemplation. The acknowledgment of this shadow was the inaugural step, but the embrace, nurtured by compassion, ignited the transformation.

Acceptance opened the gates, but compassion was the catalyst. Each emotion, once a silent whisper, found a resonating echo. Every fear, once a haunting spectre, transformed into a guiding light. In this alchemy, Maria didn't just find her shadow; she discovered an enriched self, a harmonious amalgamation of the light and dark, overt and covert, spoken and silent facets of her existence.

As acceptance and compassion intricately wove the tapestry of her internal universe, a self-awareness, as illuminating as the first rays of dawn, emerged. In this awareness, the fragments of her existence converged into a soulful symphony. The fears were not just acknowledged but understood; inadequacies were not just seen but embraced, not as impediments, but as integral notes in the harmonious melody of her holistic existence.

The emotional healing was not an event but a journey. Every step, marked by acceptance and nurtured by compassion, was a stride into spaces of internal harmony. The storms of emotional tumult transformed into serene breezes of peace. Each confrontation with the shadow, once a battlefield, morphed into a nurturing conversation – a dialogue that healed the scars and illuminated the darkened corridors of the soul.

The personal growth ensuing from this dance between acceptance and compassion is a silent yet profound revolution. In Maria's reflective silences, the discoveries were profound. Each aspect of the shadow, once a repressed entity, now stood as a pillar, contributing to the enriched edifice of her self.

The transformation isn't a transcendence from the shadow but an enriched integration. It is a dance where every step, every twirl, is a testament to the silent yet potent power of acceptance and compassion. Each emotion, thought, and aspect of the self, including those nestled in the shadow, become integral strokes in the masterpiece of the holistic self.

In this transformation, the shadow is neither a prisoner nor an adversary, but a companion. Acceptance and compassion are the silent artists weaving the masterpiece of an enriched, integrated self. In this artistry, the shadows are not obliterated but illuminated. They stand not as symbols of repression but as testimonies of a soulful integration, echoing the silent yet potent anthem of holistic existence, emotional healing, and enriched personal growth.

Forgiveness & Letting Go

Imagine finding oneself in the labyrinth of emotions, where every turn reveals a forgotten memory, a suppressed emotion, a hidden scar. It is in this intricate dance of revelation and concealment that we often meet our shadow self, veiled in the recesses of our psyche. Unearthing these buried segments of ourselves is a pivotal aspect of shadow work, and central to this exploratory journey is the act of forgiveness.

Meet Jane. A highly regarded professional, an adept social persona, but behind the polished exterior lies a terrain of emotional wounds, embittered memories, and haunting regrets. Each element constitutes the shadow that silently, yet emphatically, impacts her thoughts, actions, and interpersonal relationships. Jane's story isn't a solitary narrative. It echoes the unuttered sentiment of many who venture into the intricate path of shadow work.

Forgiveness, in this intricate exploration, isn't just an emotional release but a profound empowerment. But why does forgiveness often seem like an insurmountable mountain? Why does the soul, weary and heavy with the burden of unexpressed resentment and repressed emotions, falter at the threshold of forgiveness?

Psychological barriers to forgiveness are deeply rooted, often intertwined with the very fabric of the self that has been intricately woven by our experiences, beliefs, and social conditioning. Anger, resentment, and bitterness are not just emotional responses but formidable fortresses that guard the vulnerable self from perceived threats of betrayal, rejection, and hurt.

To forgive oneself is to tread into the space where self-judgment and criticism have long reigned. It's to confront the parts that are marred by mistakes, imperfections, and inadequacies. Each echoing the silent yet formidable voice of self-condemnation. How does one silence this tumultuous echo? How does the journey from self-reproach to self-forgiveness unfold?

Forgiving others, on the contrary, is a pilgrimage into the external world where memories of betrayals, hurts, and disappointments lie in wait, like silent sentinels guarding the gates of emotional freedom. These sentries are formidable not because of their intrinsic power, but because they are fortified by the narratives we weave around our wounds.

As Jane ventured into the recesses of her shadow self, amidst the echoes of repressed anger and silent resentments, the profound need for forgiveness emerged - not as a choice but as an indispensable pathway to liberation. The resentments, like heavy chains, bound her not just to the memories but to the incessant cycle of emotional and psychological turmoil.

The journey to forgiveness is indeed treacherous, strewn with emotional and psychological obstacles. Yet, every obstacle is surmountable. The initial step lies in the acknowledgment - a profound recognition of the chains that bind the soul to the haunting echoes of the past. In this acknowledgment, there is an unmasking, a revelation that the chains, though formidable, are not invincible.

For Jane, and for every soul that embarks upon this sacred journey, forgiveness unfolds in the silent spaces where the heart, weary yet hopeful, confronts the shadow self. It is not a confrontation marked by conflict but characterized by a profound willingness to listen, to understand, and to release.

Every suppressed emotion, every repressed resentment, is a silent cry for release. In the act of forgiveness, these silent echoes find a voice. It's a voice not of tumultuous conflict, but of serene release. Each uttered sentiment of forgiveness, whether directed inwards or outwards, is a step towards the liberation of the soul from the formidable yet surmountable fortresses of resentment, anger, and bitterness.

Forgiveness in shadow work is indeed a journey - intricate, profound, yet liberating. Each step is not just an unraveling but a reconstruction - a silent yet formidable transition from the imprisoning chains of resentment to the liberating wings of emotional and psychological freedom.

Practical Exercises and Strategies for Practicing Forgiveness

Forgiveness is not a passive sentiment but an active practice, a conscientious journey from the entanglements of resentment and anger to the liberating spaces of peace and emotional harmony. While the role of forgiveness in shadow work is profoundly acknowledged, its practice is often met with formidable barriers. Here, we introduce a series of distinct, practical exercises to engage with forgiveness in a tangible, transformative manner.

Exercise 1: The Letter of Release

Begin with a private, non-judgmental space. Let it be a sanctuary where the soul, free from the scrutinizing eyes of the world, unravels its burdens. Write a letter to yourself or to the individual associated with the pain. Let every word echo the sentiments long silenced, every sentence unveil the emotions long veiled. Don't rush; let it flow, uncensored and unmasked. In this unearthing, there's a profound release. The objective isn't sending the letter but experiencing the liberation embedded in expression.

Exercise 2: The Forgiveness Meditation

Meditation is a gateway to the internal realms where the chains of resentment are forged and can be broken. Embark upon a guided forgiveness meditation. Visualize the person or the self-part needing forgiveness. Imagine a light, illuminating the darkened corners of pain and resentment. With every breath, let this light expand, illuminating, softening, and releasing. Feel the emotions, acknowledge them, and with every exhale, release them into the expanding light.

Exercise 3: The Compassion Mapping

Forgiveness and compassion are intricately linked. Create a compassion map. Draw two circles. In one, list the pains, resentments, and angers associated with the self or others. In the adjacent circle, list the potential pains, struggles, and burdens experienced by the self or the other person during the incidences leading to pain. The objective is not justification but understanding. In this mapping, witness how understanding paves the path to forgiveness.

Exercise 4: The Ritual of Release

Symbolism is a powerful medium of expression. Create a ritual of release. It could be burning the written letter, releasing a balloon, or any symbolic act that resonates. As you engage in this act, internalize the sentiment of release. Feel the chains of resentment break, visualize the soul unburdening the weights of pain and anger. It's a symbolic yet powerful journey from entanglement to liberation.

Exercise 5: The Forgiveness Affirmation

Words have the power to heal and transform. Create a personal forgiveness affirmation. It should resonate with your internal struggles and aspirational journey to forgiveness. Repeat this affirmation daily. Let every utterance be a step towards the internalization of the sentiment of forgiveness. Feel the words, not just in the mind but deep within the soul.

Each of these exercises is tailored to foster an intimate, profound engagement with the act of forgiveness. They are not just activities but pathways, each paving the journey from the tumultuous terrains of resentment and anger to the serene landscapes of peace, liberation, and emotional harmony.

For Jane, as with many others, each exercise was not a task but a revelation. In the letter, the suppressed emotions found expression; in the meditation, the angers found release; in the compassion mapping, understanding blossomed; in the ritual, the soul experienced a tangible unburdening; and in the affirmation, the journey to forgiveness found a persistent, echoing voice.

In this intimate, personalized engagement with these exercises, the practice of forgiveness transitions from a conceptual understanding to a lived experience - a transformative journey from the shadowed spaces of resentment to the illuminated landscapes of peace, understanding, and emotional liberation.

Liberation and Healing Through Forgiveness

The intricate dance of the soul with forgiveness, winding through the pathways of acknowledgment, understanding, and release, heralds a dawn where liberation isn't just a concept, but a lived experience. In the aftermath of the tumultuous yet transformative journeys like Jane's, there is an awakening to a realm where the burdens of resentment and the chains of anger are replaced by the wings of freedom and the lightness of peace.

Forgiveness, as experienced in the silent yet profound depths of the soul, isn't an erasure of the past but a transformation of its hold on the present and the future. Each resentment released, every anger unburdened, is akin to the shedding of chains that have long imprisoned the soul in the dungeons of emotional and psychological turmoil.

In this newfound freedom, there is a silent yet profound unfolding of healing. Emotional wounds, long festering beneath the heavy cloaks of denial and suppression, are exposed to the healing touch of awareness, understanding, and release. Each confrontation with the shadowed self, mediated through the transformative power of forgiveness, is not a battle but a healing embrace.

Jane's silent tears, flowing not from the pains of confrontation but from the relief of release, echo the sentiment of liberation. In the silent spaces of the soul, where the echoes of resentments and angers once reigned, there is now a melody of peace, a harmony of acceptance, and a rhythm of freedom.

The liberation ensuing from forgiveness isn't confined to the internal realms. It extends its gentle, yet powerful touch to the spaces of interpersonal relationships. The chains of resentment and anger, long a barrier to connection, intimacy, and understanding, dissolve to unveil bridges of connection, pathways of understanding, and gates of deepened intimacy.

In this liberation, mental health is not just a clinical term but a lived experience. The mind, once a battlefield of conflicting emotions, suppressed pains, and echoing resentments, transforms into a sanctuary of peace, clarity, and balance. Mental turbulence gives way to emotional serenity, psychological conflicts dissolve into internal harmony, and cognitive dissonances transform into aligned understanding.

Jane's awakening, a testimony to the transformative power of forgiveness, isn't an isolated narrative. It's an echo of the silent yet profound revolution that unfolds in every soul that embarks upon the intricate yet liberating journey of forgiveness in shadow work. In the unburdening of resentments, there is an unfolding of peace; in the release of anger, there is an embrace of serenity; and in the dissolution of the chains of the past, there is an awakening to the freedom of the present.

In this silent yet echoing revolution, the shadowed self is neither an adversary nor a prisoner. It emerges as a companion in the profound journey of life, where every unveiled wound is a gateway to healing, every confronted resentment is a pathway to peace, and every released anger is a step towards liberation.

In the harmonious dance between the shadow and the light, mediated by the transformative power of forgiveness, the soul doesn't just confront and reconcile with the shadowed self but transcends into spaces of holistic existence, marked by emotional freedom, psychological balance, and an enriched, deepened, and liberated engagement with the self, others, and the intricate tapestry of life.

Conscious Tension Release

David was an embodiment of vigor, a picture of physical health, with every muscle and sinew an epitome of strength. Yet, there was an undercurrent, a subtle yet persistent echo of unease that defied the physical prowess and whispered the tales of an unrest, deeply ingrained and often overlooked. In the impressive architecture of his physical being, the crevices where emotions resided were often ignored, casting a shadow that silently, yet persistently, imbued his muscular strength with an inexplicable weakness.

The journey of the shadow self is often navigated in the silent corridors of emotions and psychology. Yet, the physical entity that we inhabit is not just a bystander but an intricate participant in this profound journey. The emotions, especially those repressed, unexpressed, and unresolved, do not merely float in the ether of psychological spaces but find a silent refuge in the physical body.

As David discovered, the persistent ache in his shoulders was not just a physical anomaly but an echo of repressed anger. The stiffness in his neck, a sentinel of unuttered words and unexpressed emotions. The recurrent headache, a silent rebellion of suppressed desires seeking an outlet, a voice, an expression.

Stored physical tension is the body's silent manuscript, where every ache, pain, and discomfort is a word, a sentence, a paragraph narrating the untold stories of emotional and psychological landscapes. These aren't just physical experiences but emotional narratives, each seeking acknowledgment, expression, and resolution.

In the elegant dance of existence, the body is not separate from the mind, the emotions not divorced from the physical expressions. Like a symphony, every note of emotional experience finds an echo in the physical body. The shadow self, with its repressed emotions, unresolved conflicts, and unexpressed desires, imprints itself not just in the silent spaces of the psyche but in the tangible, palpable, physical entity.

Every emotion is energy, and like water, it seeks an outlet. When denied expression, it doesn't dissipate but finds refuge in the muscles, tissues, and cells of the body. Each physical discomfort, pain, and tension is a reservoir where these unexpressed emotional energies are stored.

For individuals like David, the revelation that the body is a silent yet eloquent narrator of the stories of the shadow self is not just an awakening but a call to action. It underscores the necessity to not just navigate the emotional and psychological corridors of the shadow self but to acknowledge, address, and release the stored physical tensions that are silent testimonies of the unexpressed, unresolved emotional and psychological echoes.

As David embarked upon the intricate journey of shadow work, the exploration was not confined to the silent reflections and introspective delves into the psychological spaces but extended to the physical body. Each session of introspective reflection was complemented by a conscious acknowledgment of the physical tensions, aches, and pains.

In this acknowledgment, there was a revelation that every physical tension was a gateway, an entry point into the deeper, often uncharted terrains of emotional and psychological spaces. The persistent ache, the recurrent discomfort, each was a signpost pointing towards the repressed emotions, unuttered words, and unexpressed desires.

In the dance of shadow work, the body and the emotions are not disparate entities but intricate partners. Each physical tension is a whisper, a silent yet eloquent voice echoing the narratives of the shadow self. In listening to these whispers, acknowledging these voices, and addressing these echoes, the journey of shadow work transcends the boundaries of psychological exploration and transforms into a holistic odyssey where the body, mind, and soul converge in a harmonious dance of revelation, acknowledgment, and transformation.

Navigating the Release of Physical Tension

The potency of releasing physical tension extends beyond the immediate alleviation of discomfort—it's a doorway into profound emotional and psychological healing. In the aftermath of the practical exercises, a revelation dawns, illuminating the intricate pathways where the physical and emotional selves are not disparate entities, but intimate allies in the dance of existence.

Sarah, another soul on the arduous journey of shadow work, discovered this interconnected reality in the aftermath of conscious tension release. Each released physical tension was akin to the unraveling of a thread, meticulously woven into the intricate fabric of repressed emotions, suppressed desires, and unuttered narratives.

In the release of every physical tension, there was an echo of liberation that reverberated in the silent corridors of her emotional and psychological spaces. The stiffness in her shoulders wasn't merely a physical anomaly but a sentinel of repressed anger. As the stiffness unraveled, so did the layers of anger, revealing the wounds, the triggers, and the unuttered narratives that had long found a silent refuge in the physical bastion of her body.

The liberation ensuing from the release of physical tension is akin to the unveiling of a dam. The emotions, long repressed, find a channel of expression. The wounds, long veiled, are exposed to the healing touch of acknowledgment. And the shadows, long silent, find a voice—a voice that is not an echo of conflict but a melody of resolution.

The release of physical tension in the context of shadow work is not an isolated physical event but a holistic experience. It is characterized by an enriched self-awareness where the body becomes an eloquent narrator, echoing the silent, unuttered stories of the emotional and psychological self.

In the unwinding of every muscle, the relaxation of every tissue, there is a silent yet profound unraveling of the stories, memories, and experiences that constitute the shadow self. The body, in its majestic silence, becomes a sanctuary where the echoes of the shadow self are not just heard but acknowledged, not just seen but understood.

Sarah's tears, flowing not from the physical release but from the emotional liberation, are a testimony to the transformative power of conscious tension release. Every unveiled emotion is a step towards healing. Every unraveled narrative is a pathway to understanding. And every released physical tension is a gateway to the liberation of the shadow self.

The benefits of this intricate dance between physical release and emotional liberation are profound. Mental health is not a clinical term but a lived experience—a journey from the tumultuous terrains of conflicts, angers, and resentments to the serene landscapes of peace, harmony, and balance.

In this silent yet potent transformation, relationships transcend the boundaries of superficial interactions and morph into profound connections. The self, liberated from the chains of repressed emotions and physical tensions, engages with the world with an authenticity, a vulnerability, and a strength that is both liberating and transformative.

In the aftermath of the conscious tension release, Sarah, akin to every soul that embarks upon this intricate journey, doesn't just confront the shadow self but embraces it. In the release of every physical tension, there is a silent yet profound embrace of every emotion, every desire, and every narrative that constitutes the shadow self.

It is a dance of liberation, where every step is not a movement away from the shadow but a step towards it—a step characterized by acknowledgment, acceptance, and the profound liberation that ensues not from denial but from the embrace of every echo, every whisper, and every shadow that constitutes the enriched tapestry of the holistic self.

Processing Your Pain

As sunlight pours through a window, casting illumination, yet concurrently, shaping the contours of a shadow on the floor, so does our existence unfold, a dance of luminosity and darkness. Hannah, once a bubbly, effervescent soul, found her laughter diminishing, joy evaporating, as if a cloud, intangible yet omnipresent, cast its shade upon her existence. What was this shadow, and why did it imbibe the radiance of her life, rendering colors gray, and melodies mute?

In the silence of our hearts, amidst the cacophony of external existence, lies the shadow self—a realm inhabited by repressed emotions, past traumas, and negative beliefs. It's not a sinister entity, but rather, an intricate aspect of our holistic existence, often silent, yet echoing the unuttered, the unseen, the unfelt dimensions of our beings.

Pain, in its multifaceted expressions, is not a mere physical or emotional experience, but an intricate tapestry woven with the threads of past traumas, repressed emotions, and deeply entrenched, often unacknowledged, negative beliefs. These are not disparate threads but interconnected expressions, each influencing, shaping, and often amplifying the other.

As Hannah embarked upon the journey of introspection, a pathway not marked by the external milestones of the world but by the internal landscapes of the soul, the acknowledgment of pain associated with the shadow self emerged not as a confrontation but a revelation. Each repressed emotion was akin to a silent note in a melody, each past trauma a brushstroke in a painting, and each negative belief a stone in the pathway of her existence.

The acknowledgment of pain is an intricate dance of revelation and vulnerability, a journey where the soul, bare in its authenticity, confronts not an external entity, but the depths of its existence. It's not a battle but a delicate unfolding, where each layer unraveled reveals not a wound, but a narrative, not a scar but a story.

The psychological process of pain acknowledgment isn't a clinical diagnosis but an intimate journey. Each repressed emotion, when brought to light, loses its intimidating shadow and transforms into a vulnerable, often hurt, yet profoundly authentic expression of the self. The pain isn't an adversary but a companion, narrating the silent stories, echoing the unuttered experiences, and unveiling the unexpressed dimensions of existence.

In this acknowledgment, a metamorphosis unfolds. The pain, once a shadow casting its intimidating gloom, transforms into a vulnerable, authentic expression. Each repressed emotion, when acknowledged, begins its journey from the silent corners to the illuminated spaces of consciousness.

For Hannah, every tear shed in the acknowledgment of pain was not a symbol of weakness but a testament of strength. Each confrontation with a repressed emotion wasn't a battle but an embrace. In the vulnerable yet empowering journey of acknowledgment, the shadow self, once an intimidating entity, transformed into a silent, yet potent narrator of the untold, unexpressed, yet profoundly authentic narratives of her existence.

As we delve into the nuanced process of acknowledging the pain associated with the shadow self, we embark upon a journey not marked by battles and confrontations, but by revelations and unfoldings. Here, in the silent yet potent spaces of acknowledgment, the shadow self is neither an adversary to be conquered nor a realm to be feared, but an intimate space where the unuttered, the unexpressed, and the unrevealed dimensions of our existence await acknowledgment, expression, and integration.

The Blossoming of Resilience through Pain Processing

In the garden of the soul, amidst the thorns of pain and the blossoms of joy, a unique flower blooms—it's birthed from the soil of past traumas, watered by the tears of acknowledgment, and nourished under the sun of processing. This isn't just a flower; it's a testament to resilience, a symbol of the transformation and healing that unfolds in the intimate journey of pain processing.

Ella, a woman of profound depths, had once likened her pain to a shadowed forest, where each tree was a sentinel of a past trauma, each leaf a narrative of repressed emotions, and each breeze an echo of negative beliefs. As she ventured into the exercises of pain processing, each step wasn't just a movement amidst these silent sentinels but a dance of transformation.

Every emotion mapped, every trauma placed on the timeline, every dialogue with pain, and every reframed belief wasn't just an exercise but a silent revolution. The forest, once shadowed and intimidating, started revealing its pathways, each leading to a landscape of understanding, self-discovery, and emotional liberation.

In this transformation, resilience isn't a lofty ideal but a lived experience. It's characterized by the silent yet potent power to face, not evade; to acknowledge, not ignore; to embrace, not resist the intricate dance of pain and joy, shadow and light, repression, and expression.

With each exercise documented in the workbook, Ella didn't just pen down words but wove the threads of resilience. Each acknowledgment of pain was a strand, each processing a weave, and each acceptance a texture in the intricate tapestry of resilience.

Healing isn't a destination but a journey. In the context of shadow work, it's marked by the empowered steps where pain, once a chain, transforms into a ladder—each rung leading upwards towards the horizons of self-understanding, emotional liberation, and holistic integration.

In the aftermath of pain processing, the shadowed forest of the soul reveals its blossoms. Each flower is a narrative of pain acknowledged, processed, and transformed. The scent isn't of suppression but expression; the hue isn't of evasion but confrontation; the texture isn't of resistance but embrace.

In the narrative of shadow work, the chapter of pain processing is marked not by the echoing silence of repression but by the eloquent narratives of acknowledgment. In this narrative, each word penned in the workbook isn't just an inscription but a testament—a testament to the transformation from the silent echoes of pain to the melodious tunes of resilience.

Ella's story is not unique but universal. In the echelons of every soul, amidst the silent corridors of every heart, lies the shadowed forest. Yet, each tree is not a sentinel of imprisonment but a gateway; each leaf not a narrative of repression but a pathway; each breeze not an echo of negativity but a melodious tune leading towards the horizons where the shadow and light dance in unison.

In this dance, pain isn't a foe but a companion, each step not a movement of escape but an embrace. And in this embrace, unfolds the silent yet potent symphony of transformation, where the notes of pain compose the melodies of resilience, the tunes of self-understanding, and the harmonious rhythms of emotional liberation. In the intimate spaces of this symphony, the shadowed forest blossoms, unveiling not the thorns of pain but the blossoms of resilience, each echoing the silent yet potent narrative of transformation and healing that ensues in the profound journey of shadow work.

Transformation and Growth

Alex found himself standing on the edge of something profound. It was like the quiet before the storm, an ominous silence that promised the tumultuous yet cathartic tempest of transformation. The journey of shadow work, he would soon find, was not a venture into darkness but rather an expedition towards light – a kind of liberation that only arises when one dares to dance with the deepest recesses of their soul.

In the intricate dance of existence, where joy and pain, light and shadow intermingle, shadow work emerges as a silent yet powerful symphony of transformation. It's a dance where the steps are not choreographed but evolve, a melody not composed but unfolds, echoing the silent whispers of the soul seeking light amidst the shadows.

When Alex began the exercises documented in his shadow work journal, each line penned wasn't just an inscription but a revelation, each reflection not a mere thought but an unveiling, each acknowledgment not an end but a beginning - the beginning of a journey where the shadowed corridors of the soul echoed with the melodies of transformation.

In the silent spaces of his reflections, where the echoes of past traumas, repressed emotions, and rooted beliefs found a voice, transformation was not an event but a process. Each acknowledgment of pain, each engagement with the shadow self, each unraveling of a repressed emotion marked the intricate steps of a dance, leading from the shadowed terrains of repression to the illuminated landscapes of self-awareness and holistic integration.

Where once stood a man, a prisoner to his own repressed narratives and rooted beliefs, now stood a soul, free in its expressions, profound in its engagements, and enriched in its existence. The journey of shadow work had transformed Alex, not by eradicating the shadows but by illuminating them, not by negating the pain but by transforming it, not by suppressing the emotions but by expressing them.

In the transformative journey of shadow work, each exercise in the workbook wasn't a task but a tool, each reflection not an activity but a pathway, each acknowledgment not a conclusion but an unveiling - unveiling the intricate landscapes where the soul, liberated from the chains of repression, dances in the unison of light and shadow, pain and joy, expression, and silence.

Katie, another soul touched by the profound melodies of shadow work, narrates her transformation as a silent revolution. In the echoes of her shadow work journal, where each word was a silent note, each line a quiet rhythm, and each page a silent melody, Katie didn't just confront the shadow self but embraced it.

Where pain was a silent echo, now it was a profound expression; where the shadow was an intimidating presence, now it was a companion; where traumas were silent narratives, now they were stories - stories echoing the journey from the silent corridors of repression to the melodious landscapes of expression, acknowledgment, and transformation.

The transformative journey of shadow work is marked by the empowered steps where the soul, once a silent prisoner, emerges as a profound narrator. In the spaces of the shadow work journal and workbook, where each exercise is a step, each reflection a movement, and each acknowledgment a dance, the soul narrates its journey - a journey from the shadows to the light, from repression to expression, from the silent echoes of pain to the melodious tunes of transformation and holistic integration.

In this journey, the shadow self is neither a foe to be conquered nor an entity to be feared, but a companion, each whisper echoing the silent yet potent tunes of a transformation that unfolds in the sacred spaces where the soul, enriched in its expressions, dances to the silent yet eloquent symphony of shadow work.

Nurturing the Continuous Transformation

In the realm of shadow work, transformation isn't a destination reached but a perpetual journey, unfolding with each step taken, every breath drawn. Alex's narrative, echoed by Katie and countless others, isn't just a collection of profound revelations but a testament to the ongoing nature of this transformation. Each chapter, each sentence inked in the annals of their shadow work journal, is a step on a never-ending path that weaves through the intricate gardens of the soul, where every thorn and blossom is essential.

Strategy 1: Cultivate Mindfulness

Action Steps:

- Morning Reflection: Dedicate the first moments of your day to silence and introspection, basking in the serenity and forging a connection with your inner world.

- Mindful Practices: Incorporate practices like meditation or deep breathing exercises to foster awareness and presence, crucial for navigating the ongoing journey of transformation.

- Journaling: Maintain the habit of documenting your thoughts, emotions, and revelations, for in these inscriptions lies the map of your evolving journey.

Strategy 2: Engage with Art Therapy

Action Steps:

- Expression through Art: Allow your emotions, even the tumultuous and confronting ones, to flow into creative expressions - be it painting, music, or any form of art.

- Interpretation: Spend time interpreting your creations. Each piece isn't just art, but a narrative, a chapter of your ongoing story of transformation.

- Integration: Integrate these insights into your life, allowing them to sculpt your perspectives, actions, and responses.

Strategy 3: Form Support Networks

Action Steps:

- Connect with Others: Join groups or communities, whether online or offline, that focus on self-discovery, healing, and transformation.

- Share Your Journey: In sharing, there's amplification of insights and reflections; your narrative becomes a mirror reflecting the universal dance of shadow and light.
- Receive and Offer Support: Be receptive to insights and support, and equally, extend your learnings and strength to others navigating their journeys.

Strategy 4: Educational Engagement

Action Steps:

- Read Extensively: Dive into literature that explores the psyche, emotions, and the enigmatic dance of shadow and light. Each reading illuminates a facet of the intricate gem of your existence.
- Attend Workshops and Seminars: These are crucibles of learning and evolution, spaces where theory and practice amalgamate, offering tools for your continuous journey.
- Apply Learnings: Every piece of knowledge acquired is a tool; apply them, test them, refine them. In application, theoretical insights morph into experiential wisdom.

The ongoing nature of transformation through shadow work isn't a linear progression but an expansive evolution, akin to the blossoming of a flower that unveils petal after petal, each revealing a unique hue, texture, and essence. In this blossoming, the external metrics of progress dissolve into the profound revelations of the internal landscape where every emotion confronted, every shadow embraced, and every pain transformed, marks not an end but a new beginning.

Alex, amidst the silent echoes of his reflections and the profound inscriptions of his journal, didn't just discover the shadows but illuminated them. Katie, through her artistic expressions and narratives, didn't just confront the pain but transformed it. They, like every soul embarking upon this journey, became gardeners of their souls, where each thorn encountered marked the blossoming of a new flower, each shadow confronted revealed a new light, and each pain transformed echoed the silent yet potent tunes of an ongoing, never-ending symphony of transformation and growth.

In these strategies, each step taken, every insight gained, and each reflection penned isn't just a task accomplished but a petal unveiled in the continuous blossoming of the soul, where the shadow and light, pain and joy, confrontations, and embraces dance in unison, echoing the silent yet profound symphony of transformation through shadow work.

The Ripple Effects of Transformation on All Facets of Life

In the aftermath of shadow work, transformation seeps into every pore of existence. It's an ethereal dance, where each step of unveiling the shadow, of confronting and transforming pain, carves intricate patterns of evolution, deeply etching them into the personal, professional, and spiritual domains of life.

For individuals like Alex, the journey of shadow work isn't a solitary pilgrimage to the depths of the soul. It's a radiant expansion, where every confrontation with the shadow, every dance with repressed emotions, and every acknowledgment of pain illuminates not just the internal world, but casts its gentle, transformative glow on the external existence.

In the realm of personal transformation, relationships are the first to catch this tender light. They evolve from mere interactions to profound connections, deepened by an enriched understanding and empathy emanating from the newly discovered depths within the self. Each acknowledgment of the shadow bestows a gift – the gift of self-perception that isn't a mere reflection of the world's judgments but an intricate tapestry woven from the threads of self-realization and emotional intelligence.

Professionally, the effects are profound and tangible. Decision-making acquires a nuanced elegance, infused with the wisdom gleaned from the internal odyssey. Challenges transform from intimidating mountains into inviting landscapes, waiting to be explored, understood, and conquered. Each obstacle, each challenge is no longer a test of endurance but an opportunity – a silent invitation to unveil yet another layer of potential, capacity, and resilience fostered in the crucible of shadow work.

Spirituality, too, embraces the tender touch of transformation. The divine, often perceived as a distant, enigmatic entity, becomes an intimate presence. Each acknowledgment of the shadow, each confrontation with pain, and each dance with repressed emotions isn't merely a personal revelation, but a spiritual awakening. The sacred isn't external; it resides in the profound depths of the soul, echoing the silent hymns of unity where the self and the universe dance in harmonious embrace.

As the journey unfolds, it becomes evident that transformation isn't a static achievement but a dynamic process. The impacts are not milestones to be reached but living, breathing entities, evolving, expanding, and deepening with each step on this endless journey. In the world of shadow work, every shadow unveiled is a light realized, every pain acknowledged is a strength gained, and every emotion expressed is a step towards holistic integration.

In this world, the mirror reflects not just a face, but a soul - a soul that's not defined by the scars of the past, but illuminated by the lights of self-discovery, not constrained by the shackles of repressed emotions, but liberated by the wings of expression, and not identified by external labels, but recognized by the profound, silent, yet eloquent narrative of continuous transformation.

Here, the journey doesn't conclude, for every conclusion is a new beginning, each end a fresh start, and every destination a starting point for yet another profound, illuminating, and transformative expedition into the depths of the soul, where shadows and lights don't just coexist but dance - in silent, yet profound harmony.

Maintaining Balance

Life, as perceived through the lens of consciousness, is akin to a dance between light and shadow. Both exist not as antithetical forces but as symbiotic entities, each lending depth, definition, and dynamics to the other. In the intimate dance of existence, the conscious and unconscious mind, the light and shadow self, are profound partners, dancing to the silent tunes of harmony, contrast, and integration. It's within this dance that the complexity, richness, and profundity of human experience are birthed.

Imagine the soul as a canvas. The conscious mind, or the light self, paints with strokes of awareness, logic, and rationality. It colors the canvas with the hues of the known, the understood, and the expressed. Yet, every stroke of light is defined, not just by its inherent brightness but by the contrasting touch of the shadow, the unconscious. It's within these intricate weaves of light and shadow that the masterpiece of human existence is artfully expressed.

Yet, the dance isn't without its challenges. The conscious mind, often glorified, seeks to illuminate every corner of existence with the light of awareness. But in its zealous illumination, it sometimes neglects the profound wisdom, the silent melodies, and the untapped potentials residing in the shadows, the unconscious.

John, for instance, was a man of logic. Rationality was his compass, and consciousness, his realm. Yet, in the glaring lights of the conscious, the subtle, silent whispers of the shadow were often drowned. Emotions, intuitions, and the unexpressed were relegated to the silent corners. But within these corners, within these silent shadows, resided not just repressed emotions but untapped potentials, unexpressed creativity, and silent wisdom.

The journey of shadow work is an invitation to this dance, a call to explore not just the illuminated terrains of consciousness but the silent, profound depths of the unconscious. It's a journey of balance, where the light doesn't seek to eradicate the shadow, but to dance with it, to integrate it, to be defined and refined by it.

Yet, how does one dance with the shadow? How does one integrate the conscious and unconscious, ensuring neither is neglected, neither is overly glorified, and neither is repressed? This balancing act is as delicate as it is profound. It's a dance that doesn't seek perfection but harmony, not eradication but integration, not dominance but partnership.

For John, the realization dawned through the silent yet profound pathways of shadow work. Each step into the shadows wasn't a departure from the light but a profound partnership with it. Every emotion acknowledged, every intuition respected, every unconscious pattern unveiled wasn't a negation of consciousness but a profound enrichment of it.

In this enriched canvas of existence, where the light dances with the shadow, where the conscious mind embraces the unconscious, life transforms from a monochromatic expression of known patterns into a rich, colorful, dynamic masterpiece of unlimited potentials, unexpressed creativities, and profound wisdom.

In the subsequent sections, we will explore the pathways to this dance, the strategies to this balance, and the impacts of this harmonious integration, unveiling the art of dancing with the shadows, where consciousness and unconsciousness are not adversaries but partners, painting the rich, complex, dynamic masterpiece of human existence.

The harmonious integration of light and shadow, conscious and unconscious, is more than a psychological adjustment - it's a transformation that weaves through the very fabric of one's existence, leading to enhanced emotional intelligence, resilience, and holistic well-being.

Let's take a closer look at these impacts, imagining through the journey of an individual, Sarah, who embarked on this profound pathway of balancing the contrasting yet complementary aspects of her being.

In the world where Sarah resided post her intensive engagement with shadow work, emotions morphed from enigmatic, often overwhelming forces, into articulate messengers. Each emotion, from the ecstatic heights of joy to the tumultuous depths of despair, bore significance. They were no longer entities to be suppressed or overly indulged but were acknowledged, understood, and integrated.

Every unveiled shadow, every acknowledged emotion, enriched Sarah's emotional intelligence. Her responses were no longer reactive but reflective, not impulsive but considered. Each emotion became a bridge to deeper self-understanding, a pathway to the soul's intricate landscape painted with the elaborate strokes of varied emotional hues.

In this enriched emotional landscape, resilience blossomed. Every challenge, every adversity, became an arena of growth. Sarah was no longer a passive recipient of life's unpredictable turns but an active participant. Every challenge was met with an internal robustness, a silent yet profound strength born from the integrated dance of light and shadow. Adversities were not barricades but doorways, not endpoints but pathways to uncharted terrains of inner strength, resilience, and endurance.

Holistic well-being is another silent yet profound offspring of this balanced existence. In the integrated dance of light and shadow, the physical, emotional, mental, and spiritual aspects of existence aren't disparate entities but integrated dimensions. For Sarah, physical health was not isolated from emotional balance or mental clarity. Each dimension was a note in the intricate symphony of holistic well-being, each echoing the silent yet profound tunes of balanced existence. As we encapsulate this exploration of impacts, it's pivotal to emphasize the dynamic, evolving nature of this journey. The dance between light and shadow, conscious and unconscious, isn't a destination to be reached but a pathway to be walked, a dance to be danced, a symphony to be lived.

Sarah's journey, reflective of the collective human sojourn, was not of arrival but evolution. Each shadow unveiled, each light acknowledged, each emotion expressed, and each intuition honored, is a step in this unending dance of existence. It's a dance where each step is profound, each movement, significant; painting the canvas of existence with the rich, diverse, intricate strokes of balanced, integrated, and holistic existence. Readers, as they immerse in this journey, are invited to perceive this not as a task but a living, breathing, evolving dance of existence. It's an invitation to a dance where every step is revelation, every movement, evolution; weaving the silent yet expressive tapestry of balanced, integrated, and harmonious existence.

Finding the Path to Non-Situational Happiness

As we delve deeper into the realm of non-situational happiness, it becomes paramount to outline specific, actionable strategies that not only theorize but actualize this profound state of being. Non-situational happiness isn't an abstract concept but a lived reality, tangible in its essence and transformative in its impact. The journey from the ephemeral to the eternal, from the transient to the transformative, is carved by specific steps, each a milestone in this profound journey.

Introspection and Reflection

The foundation of non-situational happiness is laid by the silent yet profound bricks of introspection and reflection. It requires a dedicated space and time to look inward, beyond the noisy distractions of the external world, into the silent, often overlooked corridors of the internal world. Journaling can be a powerful tool in this introspective journey. The act of writing, articulating, and expressing the internal experiences, emotions, and thoughts brings clarity, insight, and understanding.

Imagine, each page of the journal becoming a mirror, reflecting the unseen, unheard, unacknowledged aspects of the soul. Every word penned is a step towards self-understanding, every sentence, a pathway to internal clarity, every paragraph, a journey to the silent realms of non-situational happiness.

Mindfulness and Presence

Another pivotal strategy is the cultivation of mindfulness and presence. Non-situational happiness is not found in the distant horizons of future achievements or past reminiscences but in the profound depths of the present moment. Mindfulness practices, meditation, and conscious breathing become bridges that connect the soul to the present moment, where happiness is not a pursuit but a lived experience.

Envisage a practice where each breath is a silent chant of presence, each moment, a lived expression of happiness, each now, a profound dance of joy. Non-situational happiness blossoms in these silent yet expressive moments of profound presence, where happiness is not searched but found, not pursued but experienced.

Gratitude and Appreciation

Gratitude, too, plays a crucial role. It's the silent yet profound alchemy that transforms the ordinary into extraordinary, the mundane into magical, the everyday into eternal. A dedicated practice of acknowledging, appreciating, and expressing gratitude for the seemingly insignificant moments, people, and experiences brings a shift. It's a shift from lack to abundance, emptiness to fullness, searching to finding.

Visualize a soul where each acknowledgment is an echo of fullness, each appreciation, a chant of abundance, each thank you, a dance of non-situational happiness. In the silent yet expressive notes of gratitude, the ephemeral transcends into eternal, the transient into transformative.

Active Engagement with the Shadow Self

Lastly, an active engagement with the shadow self enriches this journey. It's not the denial but the acknowledgment, not the suppression but the expression, not the rejection but the acceptance of the shadow self that lays the foundation of non-situational happiness. Every acknowledgment is a step towards wholeness, every expression, a journey to integration, every acceptance, a dance of non-situational happiness.

Conceive a soul that is not fragmented but whole, not divided but united, not broken but complete. In the silent yet profound dance of light and shadow, emerges the radiant, expressive, and lived symphony of non-situational happiness.

Each of these strategies is a step, not just theoretically articulated but practically lived, making non-situational happiness not a distant star but a lived sun, radiating the profound, silent yet expressive tunes of joy, peace, and contentment. Each reader is not just a passive recipient but an active participant in this profound journey from the ephemeral to the eternal, the transient to the transformative, the ordinary to the extraordinary.

A Beacon for Fellow Travelers

Dear Valued Reader,

I trust this book has offered insights and tools as you navigate the profound journey of shadow work. Every individual's path is unique, yet there's a collective strength in the shared experiences and revelations we uncover along the way.

By taking a brief moment to share your genuine thoughts and reflections on this book on Amazon, you provide a guiding light to countless others embarking on similar introspective journeys. Your voice can be the assurance someone needs to delve deeper, to seek understanding, and to embrace their transformative potential.

As an independent author, every piece of feedback holds immeasurable value. Not only does it aid the growth and refinement of my work, but it also helps fellow seekers discover resources that can resonate with their own journeys.

Each word you share is a beacon, and I cherish every perspective, be it in praise or constructive critique.

From the heart, I thank you for your time and your voice. I eagerly await your insights.

Warm regards,

Megan Walls.

Conclusion

As we close this transformative journey through the intricate tapestry of Shadow Work, remember that knowledge, in itself, is only the precursor to change. The profound insights, reflections, and exercises you've encountered within these pages serve as beacons, illuminating the path toward a more integrated, authentic self. But their true power is unlocked only when applied.

The shadows within us, once mysterious and elusive, have been revealed as opportunities – chances for profound growth, understanding, and healing. By confronting and integrating these parts of ourselves, we pave the way for a life lived in harmony, free from the chains of unaddressed traumas and repressed emotions.

The journey of self-discovery is never a linear one; it ebbs and flows, presenting challenges and triumphs alike. But equipped with the tools and insights from this workbook, you're no longer walking blindly. You have the power to shape your destiny, to transform the shadows into guiding lights that illuminate your path to wholeness.

So, what's the next step? *Action*. The strategies and techniques within this book are potent, but they require your active engagement. Harness them, mold them to your unique journey, and witness the transformation they can bring about. Every day presents an opportunity to apply what you've learned, to confront a shadow, to heal a wound, to embrace a truth.

And as you move forward, remember that every step you take, no matter how small, is a step towards a brighter, more authentic you.

About the Author

Dedicated mentor and ardent consciousness explorer, Megan Walls has journeyed through the intricate landscape of the mind, soul, and spirit to bring forth insights that resonate with those on the path to self-discovery. Navigating the depths of the psyche wasn't a deliberate choice initially for Megan; it was the organic outcome of her insatiable quest to comprehend the essence of being.

Megan's first steps into the realm of consciousness exploration began with transformative spiritual encounters. These experiences steered her towards meditation, becoming the bedrock of her daily practices. Over the years, her dedication to introspection and mindfulness allowed her to tap into elevated states of awareness. These moments of clarity revealed facets of herself previously concealed in shadows, enriching her life with renewed creativity and a profound alignment with her true self.

Witnessing firsthand the unparalleled growth and serenity that emerges from confronting and embracing one's shadow self, Megan developed a fervent drive to guide others along this transformative journey. Her approach, while rooted in experiential wisdom, is also informed by her diverse academic background.

Beyond her role as a mentor, Megan is deeply committed to her own growth and spiritual practices. Her daily rituals of meditation are complemented by yoga, allowing her to maintain a harmonious balance between mind and body. Nature serves as her sanctuary; its tranquility offers her respite and inspiration. She cherishes moments spent amidst the natural world, often accompanied by her canine companions, exploring and connecting with the Earth's vibrant energy.

www.ingramcontent.com/pod-product-compliance
Lightning Source LLC
Chambersburg PA
CBHW082104280426
43661CB00089B/850